MEMPHIS STATE UNIVERSITY PRESS

This is copy __186__
of an edition of 2,000 copies

James W. Livingood

AUTHOR

Joy Bailey Dunn

EDITOR

Charles W. Crawford

EDITOR

Tennessee County History Series

Alicia M. Horton
Assistant Editor
Tennessee County History Series

EDITORIAL ADVISORY BOARD

TENNESSEE COUNTY HISTORY SERIES

Hamilton County

by James W. Livingood

Joy Bailey Dunn
Editor

Charles W. Crawford
Associate Editor

MEMPHIS STATE UNIVERSITY PRESS

Memphis, Tennessee

Maps prepared by Reaves Engineering, Inc., Memphis, Tennessee.

Manufactured in the United States of America.

Designed by Gary G. Gore.

ISBN: 0-87870-120-6

For Alma, Jim, Jr., Dick, and Carolyn and the collectors and scribes of local lore as well as all who have listened patiently.

Acknowledgments

The preparation of any history is dependent on foundations laid by countless contributors. They gathered facts, recorded incidents, interpreted events, and assigned values to what happened. They left the written word in books, journals, newspapers, diaries, and musty old scraps of paper; they left an oral tradition in ballads and myths; and they left as evidence of their life-style examples of art, architecture, and technology. Most of these contributors to the record are anonymous but nevertheless deserve a word of recognition.

Specifically, I wish to acknowledge the aid rendered by the competent staff of the History Division of the Chattanooga-Hamilton County Bicentennial Library. I am also under obligation to some past local historians including Walter T. Wood, Jr., Robert Sparks Walker, Culver H. Smith, Creed Bates, and especially my good friend and fellow worker Gilbert E. Govan. A corps of contemporary scholars gave help including Elizabeth and Cartter Patten, David Gray, Penelope Allen, Joan Franks, John Wilson, and Albert Bowman.

I also wish to recognize certain groups whose encouragement helped in the long and solitary hours of research and writing: the Chattanooga Area Historical Association, the Chattanooga Civil War Roundtable, the staff of the Chickamauga Chattanooga National Military Park, friends at the Convention and Visitors Bureau and the Chamber of Commerce, university colleagues, the former Chattanooga Hamilton County Bicentennial Committee headed by Spencer McCallie, Jr., and Floyd Delaney, and officials from both the city of Chattanooga and Hamilton County.

A special expression of gratitude is extended to the Chattanooga Hamilton County Regional Planning Commission and especially to Martha Carver, its preservation planner, for the illustrations. They represent sites and structures listed in the National Register of Historic Places.

Funds to cover the expenses of preparing a history of Hamilton County were made available from several anonymous foundations and the Hamilton County government.

James W. Livingood
July 20, 1980

Preface

The problem of composing the rich and colorful history of Hamilton County to fit into an established formula of limited proportions is indeed a difficult assignment. What happens is not far different from the experience of a cook preparing a favorite dish in a small casserole. First the cook eliminates some of the ingredients from the recipe. Then, in pouring the preparation into the baking dish, she has some left over. Finally, and most frustrating, she spills some on the floor in moving the full casserole from the preparation counter to the oven. When cooked, what she has may or may not be tasty and nourishing, and it is not necessarily what she started to make.

The ingredients left out and that which was spilled in preparation of this book may never be known to all readers, but it is hoped that those with special interests will not be too disappointed about omissions or errors of detail or with summations that crowd out names and the interesting spice of a detailed story.

$\mathcal{H}$AMILTON County on the Tennessee River in the southeastern portion of the state has been the homeland for generations of
Tennesseans. Since 1819 this land has been called Hamilton, but for
countless previous ages no political borders or surveyors' lines
marked man's division of the earth. The rugged terrain did stimu-
late the imaginative Cherokee to develop a genesis story. One of
their sacred myths describes the land as flat, wet, and soft; the
animals, crowded far above "beyond the arch," wanted to come
down. To test conditions they sent out the Great Buzzard who tired
after its long flight. In the Cherokee country its wings touched the
land and scooped out valleys and when the buzzard turned upward,
mountains were formed. Fearing all the earth would be so disturbed,
the animals called their scout back, but the ridges and valleys remained where the Cherokee lived.

Actually the local landscape produced by the physical forces of
nature resulted from possibly 600 million years of environmental
change. For silent centuries a sea covered the area, changing periodically into soft tidal flats and swampy tangles. Numerous marine
and amphibian organisms lived and died, leaving their fossil im-
prints on limestone and shale. Vegetable debris rotted before being
pressed into veins and pockets of coal. Violence interrupted the
quiet years: the wrenching and thrusting of great quakes and the
fiery ash of volcanic eruptions altered the surface. Then came eras

1

of erosion when the softer materials were carried away to low-lying areas as time's slow pace continued.

Anticlinal ridges eventually emerged; today the rock strata of Walden Ridge and Lookout Mountain tilt upward toward former great peaks. Valleys like Lookout and Chattanooga, on the other hand, are the eroded floors of earlier heights.

Tempestuous times varying from icy cold to tropical readings along with wind and rain eroded the softer parts of the sandstone rock caps of Lookout Mountain, Walden Ridge, and parts of White Oak Mountain. Here nature left its sculptured pieces of odd dimension and shape, thus challenging the imagination of man to recognize a fairyland, a "citadel of rocks," a rock castle, or Rock City. On Walden Ridge a special natural curiosity received from old-timers the name Sunken Lake, later called Llewellyn or Montlake.

Erosion, not limited to surface features only, dissolved much underground limestone, thus creating at least 15 major caverns. The interior of Lookout Mountain is honeycombed with winding passageways and great sunken rooms; it is here that the largest cave of the county is located, recognized by the visitor as Ruby Falls Cavern.

The Land

The 587 square miles of Hamilton County lie at the southern limits of the valley of East Tennessee and possess the typical features of this geographic province. The Tennessee River virtually bisects the valley, which is framed with palisade-topped mountains and spectacular scenery. Draining a vast area marked by heavy rainfall and rapid runoff, the old Tennessee River recorded almost annual spring freshets or floods and summer shallows. Its upper reaches, like all western rivers, had many shoals, reefs, hidden ledges, and an ever-changing channel. Through the years of earth-building the river proved strong enough to maintain its old course through the uplifting mountains. To the west of Chattanooga the Tennessee met its major test as it chiseled its way through the Cumberland Plateau in a deep gorge, foregoing a direct route to the south and the Gulf of Mexico.

Flowing past the foot of Lookout Mountain, the stream cuts a tortuous outline of a moccasin before entering the mountain stretch, called the "Narrows" by oldtime rivermen and the "Grand Canyon" by later generations. On closer inspection it is the valley of whirlpools where a series of colorful names identify specific sections of the treacherous flow where the river leaves Hamilton for Marion County. Tumbling Shoals, the Pot, the Suck, the Skillet, the Pan all meant trouble for the rivermen: they made downstream journeys hazardous and restricted upstream travel severely. Thus, the Tennessee River never became a great watery highway to the west and, instead, Chattanooga developed into a kind of midway riverport and transfer site. In 1913 with the completion of Hales Bar Dam, engineers modified this river stretch, and 20 years later the hardhats of TVA created a "new" river from the "old" one.

The western border of the county rests on the Cumberland Plateau and bears the name Walden Ridge to honor a pioneer hunter. Only a few gaps penetrate the escarpment, limiting east-west travel and leaving the steep, rocky slopes and isolated coves little disturbed by settlements except for the southern tip called Signal Mountain.

Southward, beyond the deep river canyon, the northern ends of Lookout Mountain and of Sand Mountain reach into Hamilton County, the latter with such local configurations as Raccoon, Aetna, and Elder mountains. Winding valleys divide these ranges with their wooded slopes and rocky gulches. Only three miles of Lookout lie within Tennessee, where an elevation of 2391 feet and a unique shape form a landmark of distinction. Early maps labeled it "Chatanuga," a Creek word interpreted to mean "rock that comes to a point"; a Cherokee interpretation in translation means "mountains looking at each other."

The eastern boundary of the county follows White Oak Mountain in the northern part but spreads out eastward toward the south including Bauxite and Pine Hill ridges. Actually, only a prominent ridge, White Oak, is steep and rough and penetrated by relatively few passes: Taliaferro Gap, Ooltewah or Dead Man's Gap, and Collegedale Gap. East of the Ooltewah Gap a smaller elevation carries the name Grindstone Mountain.

Between the eastern and western shoulders of the county lie numerous ridges of many shapes; some are steep, some broad;

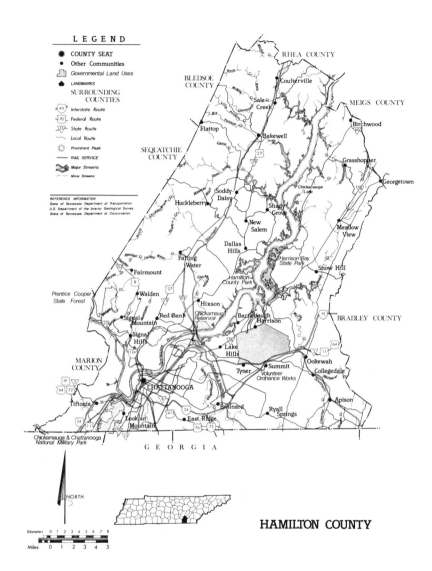

HAMILTON COUNTY

some have sharp crests; others are rounded; some are chert banks and others feature rocky spines; some are but knobs or knolls. They required the boring of rail and highway tunnels to ease travel and offered attractive sites and colorful names for real estate developments. Most run northeast to southwest with the major ones marked on the map as Bakewell Mountain, Missionary Ridge, Stringer's Ridge, Gold Point Ridge, and Godsey Ridge.

The well-watered land (average annual precipitation 51.92 inches) supports a great variety of evergreens and hardwoods with lower level growth enhanced by the blooms of dogwood, redbud, laurel, holly, and rhododendron. Naturalists have counted 551 species of wild flowers. The forests and open savannahs once sheltered the buffalo, elk, wild hogs, and passenger pigeons, but they are gone today, leaving the wild life habitat to smaller game, deer, reptiles, waterfowl, wild turkey, small birds, and a rare eagle.

Springs of cool, fresh water, once plentiful, have become an endangered species. Large and small tributaries all flow into the Tennessee River. On the right, descending the river, are Sale Creek, Possum Creek, Soddy Creek, and North Chickamauga Creek, all flowing from Walden Ridge in eye-catching cascades in the wet season and as rocky scars in dry periods. Their currents cut deep gorges through the escarpment exposing veins of bituminous coal which invited early, small-scale mining. On downstream, Mountain, Shoal, Middle, and Suck creeks join the Tennessee River.

On the left shore coming downstream, the traveler passes Grasshopper Creek, Ware Branch, Wolftever, and the Long Savannah creeks before coming to South Chickamauga, Citico, Chattanooga, and Lookout creeks. These all flow through more level country, thus offering fertile bottom lands for the pioneer farmer.

First Comers

These waterways attracted the county's first citizens, unknown in name, clan, and tribe. Most likely they were of Asiatic stock, immigrants who made their way across the Bering Sea island steppingstones and the vast North American continent. Only scattered fossils and artifacts tell an incomplete story of their residency. Since so little is known about them, archaeologists have given names to the long eras when cultural attainment was generally similar. The first ones arrived perhaps 15,000 years ago, wanderers who sought the now extinct mammoth, mastodon, sloth, and tiger. Some of their stone tools and pointed spear points found locally alone testify to the activities of these hunters of the Paleo Age.

After some 7000 years Archaic people moved in. They were a sedentary folk—really the county's first residents—who used bone, shell, and stone for making tools and ornaments. They lived in caves or crude huts but moved about quite often. Archaeologists have found evidence of a homesite on Moccasin Bend.

Much more significant were the representatives of a third cultural epoch, the Woodland Period. It started some 3000 years ago and dominated life in the area for about two millennia. The Woodland Indians raised corn, knew the art of weaving and pottery making, and used the bow and arrow. They are best known, however, for the earthen mounds they built as ceremonial burial centers. The mounds contained not only human remains but a variety of articles buried to ease the spiritual journey after death. So influential were these people in the local area that archaeologists refer to mound builders throughout East Tennessee as Hamilton Indians although only a few mounds and deserted village sites remain today.

About 1000 A.D. the Woodland culture gave way to a more advanced life-style called the Mississippian Era. The Mississippian Indians enjoyed numerous technological advances, intensive farming methods, sport at the chunky grounds, and community life centered at the mounds where civic and temple structures faced a public square. While they lived all along the Tennessee River within the county's future limits, two central areas were developed on Hiwassee Island (to the north of the Hamilton line) and Dallas Island. The latter became a focal point of "temple mound" life prior to 1300 A.D. The island, about 84 acres in size, and the two river banks comprised the site of a wilderness metropolis where the natives talked politics and war, displayed their shellcraft and ornamental arts, and celebrated their festivals and ceremonies. Their stockaded village and imposing structures have long since disappeared, and in 1940 the island itself slipped under the waters of Chickamauga Lake except for a tiny "new" island which can still be seen at the county park.

The European Connection

In June of 1540 a band of Europeans led by the Spaniard Hernando De Soto entered the Hamilton story. They came with horses, gunpowder, and tools of iron; the Iron Age directly confronted the Age of Stone. On their journey from Tampa Bay they crossed the southern mountains and struck the Tennessee River before passing through the local area. Shortly after this, another Spaniard, Juan Pardo, spent time at a fort constructed in the region. Neither De Soto nor Pardo left any positive token of his visit, but the Spanish did establish a vague claim of possession to the entire southeast, and world mapmakers painted the spot the same color as used for the powerful Iberian monarchy.

A century passed; then the English pressed claims to a vast land by chartering the colony of Carolina which extended to the Pacific Ocean. Based on little or no geographic information, they generously included all of the Tennessee country in their province and by chance placed the southern boundary on the latitude which later became the Georgia-Tennessee boundary and the southern limits of Hamilton County. Subsequently the Carolina colony was divided, and North Carolina received jurisdiction over the future Tennessee lands.

France entered the international contest about this same time, probing into the valley of Tennessee from her established claims bordering on the Mississippi River. The struggle for colonial control of the southeast naturally led to both Indian involvement and international wars. By this time tribal history had begun, and by 1715 the powerful Cherokee Nation had driven out the Creeks, Yuchi, and Shawnees. The victors had their villages in the great southern mountains with only one group, the Overhill Cherokee, living on the western slopes along the Little Tennessee, Tellico, and Hiwassee rivers. All of the Tennessee country was a huge hunting ground.

For generations no Indians actually lived in the Hamilton

County area. But Redmen used the river and followed the many old established trails first charted by the buffalo and then worn smooth and deep by the traveling tribesmen. Major traces and minor trails laced the countryside. The Great Indian Warpath entered the county in the northeast, passing through Ooltewah, over Chickamauga Creek in the Brainerd area, on to Citico Creek and around Lookout Mountain to the west. The Chickamauga Path carried warriors from north Georgia around Chattanooga and on to Kentucky while another, the Tennessee River, Ohio, and Great Lakes Trail, passed from north Georgia via Chattanooga and northward along the base of Walden Ridge. Still another major route called the Cisco and St. Augustine Trail—portions of which were known as the Nickajack Trace—ran from Florida into Middle Tennessee.

The European powers drew the Indians into their struggle for supremacy which culminated in the French and Indian War (1754–1763). To hold Cherokee allegiance the British built old Fort Loudoun on the Little Tennessee River. Here the Union Jack flew over the westernmost outpost of the men of England. Ill-treated and discouraged by their role as pawns, the Cherokee rebelled, besieged the fort, and forced its surrender on August 7, 1760, after which they ambushed and slaughtered the whites on their way back to Charleston.

Indian runners invited the French authorities at New Orleans to take possession of the fort. Although the war was going badly for them by this time, the French forwarded boats with gifts and stores which foundered at the treacherous mountain stretch of the Tennessee River. Here the mission ended, but old maps show an "Old French Store," possibly on Williams Island, where a temporary outpost apparently stood for a short time over which the French national banner flew.

The war ended in a British victory; all of southeastern North America passed to them in the treaty that followed. The Cherokee again accepted British sovereignty. When English army engineers entered the newly-acquired lands to inventory their gains, one party visited the local area and in its report used the name "Suck"—the first written record of its usage—for the rough waters of the Tennessee River in the mountain canyon.

The Chickamaugas

Fragile Anglo-Cherokee relations grew more brittle as American pioneers settled west of the mountains about 1769. The appearance of cabins in the Tennessee country not far from the Overhill Cherokee villages spelled trouble on the frontier. Moreover, land speculators schemed to buy vast tracts without thought of Indian rights or British regulations.

In March of 1775 on the very eve of the American Revolution, Richard Henderson negotiated to purchase 20 million acres; older chiefs acquiesced and terms were reached with one young minor chieftain objecting. He chided his elders about forfeiting their heritage and threatened the purchaser. In a forceful impassioned speech this Cherokee named Dragging Canoe told Henderson: "You have bought a fair land, but there is a cloud hanging over it. You will find its settlement dark and bloody."

Other dissatisfied braves rallied around Dragging Canoe and by 1777 had seceded from the Cherokee Nation. They would use the tomahawk to retain their homeland; they would roll back the frontier. By river and trail they migrated to the valley of South Chickamauga Creek. Here as a splinter tribe they were called Lower Cherokee or Chickamaugas. Dragging Canoe, joined by Creeks and Tories, became the most powerful native leader in the southeast.

There was one European living in the South Chickamauga neighborhood when Dragging Canoe's "Chickamoggy" arrived. In 1766 a young Scot named John McDonald immigrated to Charleston, South Carolina. He entered the Cherokee trade and lived in the Little Tennessee towns with the natives. There he married Anna Shorey, the mixed-blood daughter of trader William Shorey, and according to Cherokee custom was made a full member of the tribe. The McDonalds moved about 1770 to the crossing of the Great Indian Warpath over Chickamauga Creek and there operated a trading post. John McDonald was Hamilton County's first businessman.

With Britain supplying their guns and ammunition, the Chickamaugas constantly raided frontier settlements and played a key role as effective opponents of the American patriots. Before long the new governor of Virginia, Patrick Henry, recognizing the Chickamaugas as only "banditti" who burned and scalped and made use of the Tennessee River unsafe, authorized a campaign against them. With the support of the governor of North Carolina, an expedition commanded by Colonel Evan Shelby invaded the Chickamaugas's territory by a river flotilla.

On April 10, 1779, a band of 600 to 900 men embarked on a rear guard offensive along South Chickamauga Creek. The militiamen burned 11 villages and took horses and the pelts and deerskins from McDonald's post. On their way home they auctioned off some of the loot at a stream afterwards called Sale Creek. But the Chickamaugas escaped virtually unharmed. They rebuilt their homes, continued to assault distant settlements, and to control river traffic.

In the following year a large fleet appeared on the Tennessee carrying women and children to a new wilderness settlement around Nashborough. They tied up overnight at South Chickamauga Creek where Mrs. Ephraim Peyton gave birth to the first recorded white baby in the county area. The next day, March 8, the party under the leadership of John Donelson started their run through the Chickamauga-dominated area and the bad waters of the Suck.

The Chickamaugas struck: Passengers were killed or wounded from riverbank ambush; one group of 28 sailing apart from the fleet because of a self-imposed small pox quarantine fell victim and all were killed or captured. At the Suck, Indians fired from the bluffs as the frightened voyagers tried to battle the turbulent currents and jagged boulders. Cargoes had to be thrown overboard to lighten the craft. One boat stuck on the rocks; some of the occupants were shot, others captured. Two of the women, including Mrs. Peyton, jumped into the water and pried the boat free only to realize that the day-old infant was missing. The Donelson party went on but their homesites on the Cumberland River immediately were new major targets for the warring Chickamaugas. Dragging Canoe fast became a master at guerilla fighting. His warriors lay in ambush at springs, fords, portages, and mountain passes across Tennessee and into Virginia.

The Shelby campaign clearly showed Dragging Canoe that the

South Chickamauga Creek villages were vulnerable to assault from East Tennessee. Consequently, he led his people on a second trek; this time they migrated to the river section west of Lookout Mountain and beyond the future border of Hamilton County. Protected by the rocky slopes of the mountain and Walden Ridge and by the treacherous waters of the Narrows, they constructed their five lower towns. John McDonald, serving as a British agent, moved with them.

Some Chickamaugas still occupied old town sites east of Lookout, but important locally was the fact that any expedition from East Tennessee had to cross Hamilton to attack the lair of Dragging Canoe. In the fall of 1782 such a party under the command of John Sevier appeared, sponsored by the governor of North Carolina, who had authorized payment in "Continental credit," thus giving the operation official Revolutionary status.

They put the torch to some of the easternmost Chickamauga towns but came under the taunts of warriors positioned on the bluffs of Lookout Mountain. The militiamen reacted by attacking the Indians. Among the boulders and trees of the mountain they fought what was the last battle of the American Revolution before Dragging Canoe's veterans slipped away. The date was September 20, 1782—some 11 months after the British surrender at Yorktown.

The Indian conflict did not end with the conclusion of the American war for independence. For the next dozen years the Chickamaugas continued their fight to secure their homeland, supported by supplies from Spanish Florida with McDonald now serving as Spanish Agent. Again in 1788 Dragging Canoe turned back an East Tennessee assault on the shoulder of Lookout Mountain. Meanwhile parties of warriors constantly probed the Cumberland, East Tennessee, and Virginia frontiers with torch and tomahawk.

The Canoe also maintained his control of the Tennessee River traffic. In 1785 the Chickamaugas intercepted a trader's craft filled with trade goods and carrying a young Scot as a helper. They made the crew prisoners, but John McDonald rescued his countryman and encouraged him to stay with the Chickamaugas as a trader. The lad with the fresh Scottish brogue was Daniel Ross. Ross stayed on and presently married McDonald's daughter, Molly McDonald, and became, as was the custom, a member of the tribe. On October 3, 1790, his wife gave birth to their first son, John, who lived some 48 years in the area as a leader of the Cherokee Nation.

About 1790 Dragging Canoe reached the zenith of his career. Hailed as a great patriot by his followers, he was loathed by the pioneer settlers who nevertheless respected his bravery and devotion. On February 28, 1792, he died of natural causes following a victory eagle-tail dance. The Chickamaugas did not abandon their campaigns, but two years later a military party under Major James Ore destroyed the Indian bastion. Ore's expedition came out of Middle Tennessee by approaching the Chickamauga towns through the back door and not from the Hamilton lands. It came, also, in defiance of the United States Indian policy but nevertheless brought an end to the era of the Chickamaugas.

The Cherokee

Peace talks at the Tellico Blockhouse across the Little Tennessee River from the remains of Fort Loudoun reunited the Cherokee Nation which in the next decades emerged as one of the most progressive Indian tribes within the United States. The growing pressure of white settlements and the sale of the land eventually forced all of the Cherokee to move west of the Appalachian Mountains. A continual migration to the southwest ensued. Thus Hamilton County, North Georgia, and parts of Alabama became major Cherokee territory in the early nineteenth century.

A census in 1825 placed their number at 13,563 natives, 147 white men, 73 white women, and 1277 Negro slaves. Most lived in log houses while a few owned elaborate plantation homes. The younger ones dressed like the Americans but did wear turbans. Many had good incomes by working as farmers, traders, livestockmen, and craftsmen. They conducted their business with the United States government at Southwest Point (Kingston) until 1807 when activity moved to the Hiwassee Garrison near the mouth of the Hiwassee River. For many years following 1801 the agent was Return Jonathan Meigs. In 1802 Meigs appointed William Lewis Lovely subagent; he moved to the mouth of Lookout

Creek as the first resident United States official in the county's history.

The Cherokee's progress in part stemmed from annuities which were conditions of land sale treaties. Farm implements and household utensils together with equipment for blacksmith shops, grist and saw mills, and cotton gins provided an economic base for advancement. Then in 1805 the Cherokee agreed to the construction of roads through their land, which opened the gateway to the south. One portion of the Georgia Road into Middle Tennessee, called the Nickajack Road, came around the end of Lookout Mountain and through the Rossville Gap to the main junction point at Spring Place, Georgia. Great wagons loaded with produce and herds of horses, mules, cattle, and hogs as well as flocks of turkeys made their way to Deep South markets over this first vehicular highway in the region.

Along the road across Hamilton County mixed-blood Cherokee took advantage of the new economic prospect. John Brown erected a two-story log tavern where the road met the trail to the north close to Brown's Ferry. Daniel Ross moved to a plantation on Chattanooga Creek; he had a farm, mill, deerskin tannery, large orchards, and a "well-framed house" where social life centered. John McDonald settled at the Rossville Gap, doing a large-scale business where he was later joined by his grandson, John Ross. In 1817 John Ross was appointed postmaster of the newly established Rossville post office. At that date no one knew that the McDonald enterprises came under the jurisdiction of Georgia.

Young John Ross had other interests by this time. About 1815 he and a brother, Lewis, undertook a landing and ferry service where future Chattanooga would grow. It was not an elaborate enterprise, being described by a traveler as a "kind of shanty for goods and a log hut for the ferryman."

As the Cherokee Nation moved away from a hunting economy to one of settled interdependence, missionaries also contributed to their developing life-style. Moravians, Presbyterians, and Methodist missionaries offered religious and educational instruction. But outstanding work materialized from the presence of representatives of the American Board of Commissioners for Foreign Mis-

Brainerd Mission Cemetery. The mission served the Cherokee Indians
from 1817 to 1838.

sions, an interdenominational society—Congregationalists, Dutch
Reformed, and Presbyterians—based in New England. Their
interest in missionary work among the Cherokee culminated in the
establishment of the Brainerd Mission in 1817.

Representatives of the society received federal encouragement
and funds in establishing a mission school. The Cherokee were
receptive, expressing special interest in vocational education. For
$500 the mission people bought some 25 acres of cleared land, the
original property of McDonald, along South Chickamauga Creek.
Realizing that the original name Chickamauga was badly over-
worked in this area, they renamed the school Brainerd Mission to
honor a missionary to New England Indians a century earlier.

For 21 years devoted men and women labored at the school,
which visitors say had from 80 to 100 students. On Sundays whites,
reds, and blacks worshipped together. A graveyard which occupied a "corner of the orchard next to the schoolhouse" alone
marks the spot today, but during its heyday Brainerd experienced

exciting times. Unable to meet growing demands from the Cherokee, the Mission developed as many as ten sub-mission stations in the tri-state area. May 27, 1819, was a red-letter day: U.S. President James Monroe and his party stopped to visit. He reported pleasure in what he found and pleased those in charge by suggesting that certain buildings be constructed at public expense.

The people at Brainerd early recognized the significance of the unusual work of the mixed-blood George Gist (better known as Sequoyah). This sensitive man, without formal training, came to recognize the importance of written language and determined to develop a Cherokee syllabary. Taunted and discouraged by many during his years of toil, Sequoyah persisted, and in 1821 submitted his findings to the Nation. His simple written forms of 86 characters made it possible for the Cherokee to read and write in their own tongue. He is the only man known to have accomplished a literary feat of this magnitude.

The missionaries encouraged Sequoyah; they had type cast and acquired a printing press, underwriting the cost until the Nation could pay. Biblical materials, hymnals, and religious tracts found their way into print in Cherokee. On February 21, 1828, the first issue of the *Cherokee Phoenix* appeared, a bilingual newspaper edited by a former Brainerd student. In addition to this national newspaper the Indians also produced a written constitution and in 1828 inaugurated John Ross as first Principal Chief.

At the capital, deep within Georgia, Ross faced serious problems. The pioneers' hunger for Indian lands was never satisfied. Georgia, anxious to develop trade routes with Middle America via the Tennessee River, wanted passage through Cherokee territory. Gold recently discovered spawned fresh greed and new pressure for Indian cessions, and the written constitution with its democratic republican features caused even more serious concern. It focused attention on the question as to who held sovereign power—the federal government, the state, or the Indians.

Georgia, dissatisfied with the hearing it received in Washington, acted on its own to get rid of the Cherokee. It passed a law to become effective June 1, 1830, confiscating Cherokee land and denying the Cherokee the rights of contract, of assembly, and of civil liberties. This legislation signaled an era of lawlessness in the

Cherokee lands as whites sought to anticipate the results of the law. Individual Indians, losing their property and homes, moved over the line into Tennessee; they relocated their capital in Bradley County.

Finally, an agent of the federal government managed to get a treaty of removal, the Treaty of New Echota, signed by a few Indians in December of 1835. It required the removal of all Cherokee to land beyond the Mississippi River within two years. Only 20 Cherokee signed, none of whom were officials of their government, and only two prominent men lent their names to the document. It was later ratified by the U.S. Senate by a margin of one vote.

During these years John Ross, although only one-eighth Cherokee, opposed removal as Dragging Canoe had opposed land cessions, but Ross used entirely different methods. The Canoe fought to preserve Indian rights with gun and tomahawk; Ross used the law and passive resistance. When he got little satisfaction from President Andrew Jackson, Ross turned to the courts. In a Supreme Court ruling, certain Georgia laws were declared unconstitutional; the Cherokee celebrated, but the President refused to enforce the court's decision. Ross's government took no part in the Treaty of New Echota and petitioned Congress to the effect that it did not represent the Indian government or the will of the people. The policy of passive resistance had almost total support.

The federal government sent troops to the area claiming they were there to prevent Indian disorders, but it was soon apparent that it was the Cherokee who needed protection. Ross labored constantly to reverse the removal decision by making many strenuous journeys to Washington. Meanwhile the authorities selected the Cherokee Agency, Gunter's Landing, and Ross's Landing as centers from which the Cherokee would be taken west.

At Ross's Landing a large military camp and barracks were built on Citico Creek and rough accommodations for the Indians grew up about Indian Springs at the foot of Missionary Ridge. A motley crowd poured in; some were contractors to haul goods and people, some providers of foodstuffs, some brazen swindlers, and some just ready to buy at their own price any household goods and livestock the Cherokee had to leave behind.

Ross's Landing, the site where Chattanooga had its beginnings as a ferry crossing and warehouse. Established about 1815 by John and Lewis Ross, it long catered to the river trade after the removal of the Cherokee. Today the site is used as a park.

On March 3, 1837, 11 flatboats crowded with 466 Cherokee left the Landing for the West; a second group soon started on an overland trek. Ross's policy of passive resistance proved most successful, and by the expiration date for voluntary removal only about 2000 had gone, so the United States dispatched some 7000 troups under General Winfield Scott to forcibly finish the removal.

Opposition continued; the Indians made no move to comply with Scott's orders and the soldiers took up rifles and bayonets to round them up in concentration camps. On June 6, 1838, a small steamboat with six flatboats pulled away from Ross's Landing with a band of banished natives. Soon a second river party started as well as a group who went by wagon or on foot. These midsummer departures led to an extremely high mortality rate, and Chief Ross proposed a suspension of removal until fall and petitioned for the right of the Cherokee to supervise it. Scott agreed. At the Brainerd

Williams Island. Located in the Tennessee River about five miles below Chattanooga, it was the home of numerous early Indians. *Courtesy of*

Mission the last communion was celebrated on August 19, 1838, as most of the missionaries prepared to make the long journey westward with their people. In the fall the remaining 13,000 Cherokee assembled at Rattlesnake Springs (near Charleston, Tennessee) for their melancholy journey recalled in history as the Trail of Tears.

The County's First Years

Naturally the interest of the whites in land and in settlement preceded the removal of the Indians. Actually, the preliminaries of the history of Hamilton County date back to North Carolina's ownership of the Tennessee country. At the close of the American Revolution that state's politicians and land speculators, often the same persons, maintained that the Cherokee had sacrificed ownership of the land for being on the losing side in the war.

The North Carolina Legislature agreed to transfer land title to individuals in the entire area whether it was open to pioneer settlement or closed for Indian occupancy. So the oldest Hamilton County land grant covering a large chunk of property went to Martin Armstrong and Stockley Donelson in 1788. Within a short time virtually all of the county north of the Tennessee River, with the exception of the mountain area, was legally private property, with one tract as large as 20,000 acres. Much of the language of the grants was very casual: one read, "beginning at two ashes on a Rocky bluff near the mouth of a Spring branch. . . ." This ambiguous wording together with inferior surveying instruments and techniques meant plums for future lawyers.

The federal government, having assumed guardianship over the Indians, planned to delay opening new lands in the Indian country and to restrain settlement. People with claims that could not be used in the Indian area and Tennessee politicians both worked for an opposite purpose. Whenever a new local governmental unit was established, it was given extensive borders reaching into Cherokee country as a stratagem for future claims. So from 1796 to 1801 the territory of Hamilton County fell within the farflung boundaries of Knox County. From 1801 to 1807 it was within the newly-created county of Roane and in 1807 was carved

Brown House, on the Georgetown Pike near Ooltewah. This one-story brick house, built about 1828, belonged to James Brown, prominent leader of the Cherokee Nation.

off to be a part of Rhea County with its county seat at Washington. All the while, Hamilton was closed to pioneer settlement.

The southern border of Rhea County was the Indian Line established by the purchase of 1805, which ran due west from the mouth of the Hiwassee River. The only whites south of this line were licensed people living with the Cherokee as artisans. This line, however, was south of the Sale Creek Valley and a number of families moved to this sector when Rhea County was established.

The United States acquired additional Cherokee lands by the Calhoun Treaty of February 27, 1819, including the acreage between the Indian Line and the Tennessee River. In October of that year the Tennessee Legislature organized this territory as Hamilton County, named for the former secretary of the treasury. All this region was now open for settlement except for six reservations granted to Cherokee who had made improvements at certain sites. David Field's reservation was opposite Williams Island; John Brown's place, below Moccasin Bend; William Brown's plantation, a mile west of the mouth of North Chickamauga Creek; Richard

Timberlake's land along this same stream; Judge James Brown's reservation was located where the public road crossed this stream; Fox Taylor's survey opposite Dallas Island. All these special reservations, each 640 acres in size, were held by mixed-blood Cherokee.

Just prior to the survey of the Hamilton County borders—a task which undoubtedly meant much improvising by the survey team—another future county line was drawn. In 1818 commissioners representing Tennessee and Georgia assembled to mark the 35th parallel dividing the two states. One member of the Georgia team, believing the work faulty, made another unofficial survey, concluding that the line drawn was about one-half mile too far south. The border has remained as first drawn, but arguments have boiled up over the years about this matter which gave Hamilton County additional acreage and, according to Georgians, deprived them of considerable Chattanooga tax money.

From 1819 until 1838 the Tennessee River in this area was the dividing line between Hamilton County and the Cherokee country. In 1833 after Georgia brought pressure on the Cherokee, Tennessee moved to extend its jurisdiction to the state's southern border. To do this the counties immediately north of the Tennessee River were instructed to extend their limits on the south shore to the state line. Although the law directed that the Cherokee maintain sovereignty in this area and that it continue to be closed to whites, the directive provided for a major future enlargement of Hamilton County as soon as the Indians were gone.

The 1819 law establishing the county listed Robert Patterson, Charles Gamble, and William Lauderdale as commissioners to launch the government and select a site for the county seat. As was the custom, court met at first in taverns or homes before it was located permanently on the farm place of Asabel Rawlings, first clerk of the county court. It was called Hamilton County Courthouse and in 1822 Rawlings became its postmaster. Interestingly, the seat of justice stood on leased land which was part of the original Fox Taylor reservation. Later the name of the community was changed to Dallas.

Dallas, now under the waters of Lake Chickamauga, never prospered, for in 1840, as the result of a referendum, the county seat was moved across the river to the newly-created town of Harrison where a substantial brick courthouse was erected.

In 1820 the county reported a population of 821 including 39 Negro slaves and 15 free blacks. The great majority lived in the Sale Creek area and merely transferred from Rhea County records when the new county line was established. The census figures increased rapidly in the next 20 years:

	Total	*Negro slaves*	*Free blacks*
1830	2276	115	25
1840	8175	584	93

Most of the first comers were of Scotch-Irish lineage with a few people of English, Irish, or German stock. Practically all moved from neighboring Rhea and Bledsoe counties or from places up-river using the Tennessee River to carry their homemade boats to their new homes. A sufficient number had had experience in public office, in organizing schools and churches, and in building public roads, which aided in getting a new society organized.

Clusters of cabins represented the more densely settled regions around Sale Creek, Dallas, Mountain Creek, Soddy, and Hixson. Walden Ridge was isolated. Legend has it that the pioneer on the mountain, a party named Miles, sought seclusion to avoid an Indian feud. He loaded the family household goods on a wagon and started up Levi Gap. He got stuck at the palisades because he could not negotiate the steep grade. With the common sense with which he was well-endowed, Miles took the vehicle apart and carried it to the top, piece by piece, wheel by wheel. Near Lone Oak he built a cabin. One day another oxen-drawn wagon appeared, driven by a fellow named Winchester. He had journeyed along the top of the mountain all the way from Kentucky. He and his family also settled, and the Miles clan had neighbors.

Early Hamiltonians lived on small farms where both frontier abundance and much hard work were common. Those who had slaves owned but a few and had close relationships with them. Several general stores, some grist mills, blacksmith shops, and one cotton gin along Soddy Creek were the day's specialty shops. Here and there community structures, small log houses, served as church and school. Early subscription schools, operated for short

Pleasant Matthews House at Georgetown. This two-story frame house of simple design was built between 1846 and 1855.

terms by poorly paid teachers, gathered neighborhood students at such spots as Robert Paterson's, Asabel Rawlings's, James McDonald's, and near Archibald McCallie's and "Clift's stillhouse."

Numerous pioneer families had former associations with the Methodist and Presbyterian churches on other frontiers. They reestablished services in their new homes often with improvised shelter and clergy about which scanty records exist. The Reverend Mathew Donald ministered to Presbyterians at Sale Creek, and at Soddy the Mount Bethel Church with the Reverend Abel Pearson, pastor, was organized in December of 1828. Possibly the earliest Methodist chapel, known as the Prairie Springs Meeting House and later Jackson's Chapel, was a log structure on Prairie Creek near Dallas where the pastor John Bradfield was recognized by the great shawl he always wore. Baptist and Cumberland Presbyterian congregations also organized and numerous camp meeting grounds became scenes of summer worship.

Whatever money first settlers had available was usually invested

Brown's Ferry Tavern. Built for the Cherokee John Brown in 1803, the tavern served travelers going through the Cherokee Nation. It still has its original logs and chimneys and is now the home of the Herschel Franks.

in land. Many absentee owners who held North Carolina grants either wanted to sell or lost their title for want of tax payments. Many large tracts sold for unbelievably low prices: Richard Waterhouse, for example, got 220 acres for $2.20, which when platted, was a stretch of river land one acre wide and 220 acres long. Two major real estate promoters were the brothers-in-law William Clift and Robert C. McRee of Soddy. In addition to valley lands, they took advantage, as did others, of the state's sale of Walden Ridge property in 1823 at prices ranging from 12½ ¢ to 1 ¢ an acre.

South of the River

As preparations for the removal of the Cherokee proceeded after the removal treaty of 1835, whites began to drift across the Tennessee River to gain choice occupancy rights. Although this was illegal, no one at the time appeared to care about enforcing the law. Naturally they concentrated at Ross's Landing where a detachment of troops and groups of private contractors had gathered in the removal process.

The Landing had recently assumed importance for another reason. In 1828 a small steamboat, the *Atlas,* made its way up the river over Muscle Shoals, through the Narrows beyond Ross's Landing, and on to Knoxville. A new age of travel began. Small craft, despite the difficulties of navigation, opened a market for the isolated valley farms of East Tennessee. Because of the difficult mountain stretch of the stream, these steamboats often sought out Ross's Landing as a port of entry. Moreover, this development gave added meaning to Georgia's interest in opening a gateway to the Tennessee Valley. On December 21, 1836, the Georgia Legislature authorized the building of a railroad northward from the central part of the state. Although no northern terminal for this radically new method of transportation was announced, Ross's Landing was a likely site.

The squatters who moved across the river to Ross's Landing early learned that their hunches were correct. All the land south of the river became state property; the Ocoee Land District was created and the district surveyed. Then Tennessee developed policy for transferring the land to private ownership. This scheme

Bluff Furnace of the East Tennessee Iron Manufacturing Company. The archaeological site is listed on the National Register; the pre-Civil War furnace was dismantled during the conflict.

Hiram Douglas House, on Snow Hill Road near Ooltewah. A one-story brick house constructed in 1851 by a leading frontier minister of the Cumberland Presbyterian Church.

authorized occupancy rights (those on the spot had the first option to buy) and a graduated price: if a given acreage did not sell at a given price, the price was lowered according to a fixed time table until it was available after 19 months at 1 ¢ per acre.

Some of the early arrivals included Daniel Henderson, Allen Kennedy, Albert S. Lenoir, Samuel Williams and his sons, and John P. Long. Long and his family arrived by riverboat from Washington in Rhea County in April of 1836. He opened a general store, became the first postmaster of the Ross's Landing office on March 22, 1837, and bought real estate. Long put his thoughts about his new home on paper. As a businessman, he saw it as a place where the corn and cotton country met. "Upon further examination," he wrote, "I found here all the requirements to build a future city." So he simply built a "log cabin in the woods and settled down for life."

Others joined these citizens, most coming to the Landing from neighboring counties. In 1838 Ferdinand Parham and his family drifted down the Tennessee. Being a journalist, he stowed away on board with his household goods and heirlooms a printing press and type. Parham tied his craft by the river bank under a comfortable shade tree and got out the first edition of the *Hamilton Gazette* on July 19, 1838.

Chattanooga

Newsman Parham found his new home a busy place. In addition to the last exciting days of Indian removal, there were steamboat arrivals. The 53 heads of households living in the area banded together to make land entry at the Cleveland office easier and appointed commissioners to represent them. Those founding fathers were Allen Kennedy, Albert S. Lenoir, John P. Long, Reynolds A. Ramsey, Aaron M. Rawlings, and George W. Williams.

The commissioners entered the land and then hired surveyors to lay out the town, which comprised about 240 acres. It was bounded by the river and Ninth Street and by Georgia Avenue and Cameron Hill. To their everlasting credit, they made the main street very wide. The commissioners then prepared deeds for those with occupancy rights and designated certain lots for the future use of churches.

They next called a public meeting to consider a name for the new community, for Ross's Landing was too limiting for their dreams for the future. The name Chattanooga, the Indian name for Lookout Mountain, was debated. Some held the word "uncommon," "uncouth," and readily mispronounced. But others agreed that it would become "familiar" and "pleasant" and that if their town prospered, "there would not be another name like it in the world." Following the vote in favor of the new place name, the post office renamed Ross's Landing Chattanooga on November 14, 1838, and editor Parham's newspaper became the *Chattanooga Gazette.*

On April 20, 1839, the commissioners sold at auction the town lots not taken by those with occupancy rights. Some of the original settlers added to their holdings and newcomers Dr. Milo Smith, James A. Whiteside, Thomas Crutchfield, Sr., John Cowart, and others got home or business property. Land near the river brought the best prices and by day's end some $45,000 had been realized.

By this date land in the Ocoee District outside of Chattanooga had gradually declined in price so that it also was attractive to investors. John P. Long bought; Thomas Crutchfield, Sr., acquired larger holdings; James Whiteside got extensive acreage on the summit of Lookout Mountain; and, the state of Georgia purchased a large tract immediately south of Ninth Street for its railroad yard and other facilities. A syndicate of investors from various parts of the southeast represented locally by Samuel and George Williams and Whiteside purchased land, for they believed that the Georgia railroad terminal would be Chattanooga.

On December 20, 1839, the Legislature completed local arrangements by passing an act "to establish the town of Chattanooga . . . and to incorporate the inhabitants thereof." James Berry, another former Rhea County man, became first mayor. The village of Chattanooga was an urban frontier. Small, straggly, and hastily built, it contained much open space, a kind of garden town where residents raised truck and kept poultry and livestock. But it did present the possibility for some economic specialization: lawyers, merchants, doctors, draymen, craftsmen, and others gave expression to their talents and special interests. Social cooperation was easy compared to rural districts, and clubs, churches and schools started early. In addition, new ideas circulated, some originating with residents born in foreign countries, some with visitors or travelers from the world of business. For a decade or so the community livelihood centered on the activity at the Landing where log rafts, flatboats, and steamers moved. But the future rested on the completion of the railroad.

Rail Junction

The Western and Atlantic Railroad ran its first through train into Chattanooga on May 9, 1850, from Atlanta with connections to Charleston, South Carolina, and Savannah, Georgia. This 137-mile rail connection was the first in the country to reach a tributary of the Mississippi River. It called for a major celebration in which Atlantic Ocean salt water was poured into the Tennessee River accompanied by cheers for the state of Georgia which financed, built, and operated it.

Although railroading was new and untried, the local effect was stimulating and unexpectedly diverse. Freight shipment south, it was claimed, was immense. Since the rolling stock was limited, farm products, flour, whiskey, and cotton piled up at the wharf and along some of the streets. The number of forwarding merchants increased to eight by 1853. Coal, shipped in boxes and barrels to blacksmiths in the Deep South, entered the trade from Sale Creek and Soddy mines. Livestock also arrived at the railhead in large numbers awaiting shipment.

The railroad gave new life to the river trade. The packets, now more like feeders than through carriers, crowded the landings. Chattanoogans James and William Williams managed one of the largest fleets while William served as mayor and president of the first bank in town. The railroad also sparked real estate interest in Walden Ridge and spurred on the completion of the Anderson Pike over this mountain from the Sequatchie Valley so that the farmers of the valley could get to the southern markets.

Passenger travel took on new meaning although the service was not always good and the accommodations were uncomfortable. Tourism began as an economic venture as people from the lower South sought escape in the mountains to avoid humid summers and deadly epidemics. In 1852 James A. Whiteside, one of Chattanooga's greatest promoters, led a group in building a toll road up Lookout Mountain and four years later opened the Lookout Mountain Hotel. A gazetteer in 1860 called the mountain a "noted summer resort."

A major hotel catered to the traveler in town. In the late 1840s Thomas Crutchfield, Sr., built a hostelry across the street from the depot. This three-story inn became the social, economic, and political center of the community as the hub of business moved from the river landing to the railroad station. On November 5, 1851, the success of Chattanooga and the optimism about the future caused the Legislature to change its official designation from "town" to "city." Soon afterward the corporate borders were moved about one-half mile to the south and east.

The most significant result of the completion of the Western and Atlantic Railroad was the encouragement it gave other rail enthusiasts to build connecting roads. In 1845 the Legislature authorized the building of the Nashville and Chattanooga Rail-

Read House. Built on the site of the pre-Civil War Crutchfield House in 1871 and reconstructed in 1926, the hotel carries on the tradition of a gracious hostelry.

road; this 151-mile line was finished in February of 1854 after the completion of the long river bridge at Bridgeport, Alabama. It opened coal fields on the Cumberland Plateau and immediately found local interests engaged in mining at Aetna Mountain.

On March 28, 1857, the last spike was driven on the Memphis and Charleston Railroad which actually operated between the Mississippi River city and Chattanooga. To eliminate expensive construction costs around Lookout Mountain, the officials of the company worked out an arrangement with the Nashville company to use common tracks from Stevenson, Alabama, into Chattanooga.

Through East Tennessee two companies finally completed routes by 1855; the southernmost, the East Tennessee and Georgia, connected Knoxville with Dalton, Georgia. To provide a more direct route for trains connecting with the west and north, a short cut was built from Cleveland to Chattanooga. In 1858 with the completion of the Missionary Ridge tunnel, service with the cities of the northeast was assured. Another route reaching Meridian, Mississippi, was planned, and in 1860 the Wills Valley Railroad, 14 miles in length, ran from Wauhatchie to Trenton, Georgia.

In the decade of the 1850s Chattanooga emerged as a major rail junction town in the South. Railroad travel, so new and experimen-

Conner Toll House on Signal Mountain. This recently restored log cabin was a toll house on the "W" road on top of the mountain beginning in 1858.

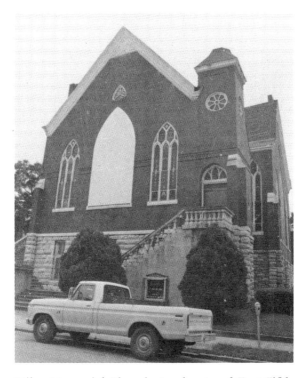

Wiley Memorial Church, Lookout and East Fifth streets. This site has been used for religious purposes since 1838. Blacks bought the damaged postwar church and in 1886 the congregation launched the building of the current Gothic Revival structure.

tal, represented the most advanced technology of the time. All the roads into Chattanooga were relatively short; this was typical, but locally the important factor was that all used the same gauge. Moreover, they built cooperatively a union depot. From a local standpoint it is interesting to note that all crossed Hamilton County south of the Tennessee River; there was not a single mile in the older part of the county.

The census takers in 1860 found 13,258 people in Hamilton County of whom 192 were free blacks and 1419 slaves. Of the total

Brabson-Loveman House. The original structure, built in 1857-1858 by Congressman Reese Brabson, served as a Civil War hospital and headquarters. Destroyed by fire in 1881, it was rebuilt and became the property of the D. B.

St. Paul's Episcopal Church. Built in 1886-1888, this church accomo-
dates a congregation organized in the 1850s; it is considered to be the
mother parish in this area.

residents, 2545 lived in Chattanooga. The population was very
young. More than one-half were Tennessee natives although 25
different states were given as birth places. At least 12 foreign
countries were places of origin. The Irish, the most numerous
ethnic group, were largely railroad workers, the Germans craftsmen, and the English mechanics and iron artisans.

Throughout the county most of the men gave their occupations
as farmers or farm laborers: a number of women were listed as
heads-of-families while some were identified with the term
"housewifery." There were 22 industries in Hamilton County, of
which most were Chattanooga businesses, employing 210 men and
four women. They turned out products with an annual value of
just under $400,000.

The majority of the plants were in or near Chattanooga. Most
were industries which prepared a relatively simple process on a raw

Locomotive 4501

Asbury United (Highland Park)
Methodist Church

material—flour mills, distilleries, tanneries, lumber mills, and meat packing establishments. More complex processes marked the iron industry. In 1860 Webster & Mann made stationary and portable engines and boilers. S. B. Lowe operated the Vulcan Iron Works. At the bluff near the river landing a modern blast furnace, with which such local men as James A. Whiteside and Robert Cravens were associated, undertook progressive experiments in 1860 to use coke in the smelting process.

The census disclosed an interesting group of professional people. The county reported 18 lawyers only two of whom were over 40 years of age, two druggists, one dentist, about 40 teachers, 30 doctors including an 18-year-old girl, and at least 20 clergymen representing the Baptist, Catholic, Cumberland Presbyterian, Methodist, Presbyterian, and Protestant Episcopal churches.

The churches received some assistance in their moral crusades from the city government of Chattanooga. Ordinances representing the conscience of the day and a desire to supplement slave

codes filled the record books with blue laws prohibiting Sunday
work as well as Sunday gaming, restricting slave assemblies, regis-
tering free blacks, and calling for fines for indecent dress and "rude
and indecent or profane discourse."

No tax supported schools existed, but a number of subscription
schools came and went. Representative ones in the 1850s included
Masonic Female Institute, Select School, and Aldehoff's in the
Chattanooga area along with Hamilton Male Academy, Alpine
Academy, and Fairmount Academy on Walden Ridge, Hamilton
County Male Academy at Harrison, and Sale Creek Academy.

Hamiltonians in 1860 were not a very affluent people. Only 43
persons owned real estate in property and slaves valued at $15,000
or more; of these merely 10 reported more than $40,000. The
same census gave only 32 persons who owned personal property
valued at more than $15,000.

In the Ocoee District beyond the limits of Chattanooga, the
residents experienced in the decades following 1838 similar developments and lifestyles as the people north of the river did after
1819. It was a rural society living close to the soil and the rhythm of
the seasons. Clusters of homes centered about Birchwood, Harrison (the county seat), Tyner, Chickamauga, and Silver Dale. Representative pioneer families included the Blyths, Gotchers, Igous,
Shepherds, Tyners, Varnells, and Yarnells.

The Great Dispute

The two local newspapers took opposite positions in regard to
the growing secession question although no special problem had
arisen over the issue. In the presidential election of 1860 Hamiltonians voted 1074 for John Bell, Tennessee's favorite son; 820 for
John C. Breckenridge; and 165 for Stephen A. Douglas. Lincoln's
name was not on the ballot.

The victory of the Republican candidate did not create any
major stir in Hamilton County; most people, realizing that the
Republicans did not control Congress, advised that Lincoln be
given a chance. But South Carolina embarked on a course of
secession and on January 19, 1861, Georgia followed, leaving
Hamilton County's southern boundary the dividing line between

an independent state soon to join the new Confederacy and the United States. Deep division began to surface.

At this time Jefferson Davis arrived in Chattanooga on his way home to Mississippi after having resigned from the U.S. Senate. He agreed to speak briefly to a gathering at the Crutchfield House. After his remarks, William Crutchfield, a brother of the proprietor and an outspoken Union man, quarreled with Davis's position and accused him of being a traitor. Confusion reigned; pistols were cocked before Crutchfield left. Word spread that Chattanooga was a Union town.

In a statewide referendum on February 9, 1861, Hamilton Countians voted 1445 against any plan to consider secession and 445 for. Tennessee's decision likewise opposed secession. But after the firing on Fort Sumter in April the government of Tennessee edged closer to joining the Confederacy and made specific military plans. A second referendum was set for June 8. East Tennessee Union men called a convention to meet on the eve of this balloting and Hamilton County sent 24 delegates. While the Union people organized, Confederate volunteers—the Hamilton Grays and the Marsh Blues—went off to war in Virginia.

In the referendum Tennessee voted in favor of secession. Hamilton County, like most counties in the eastern part of the state, rejected this decision 1260 to 854 with the majority of the secession votes cast in Chattanooga where secession won. The county with its two neighbors Bradley and Marion were the southernmost counties in the United States that stood loyal to the Union. Delegates again attended the East Tennessee Unionists' gathering, although they could not anticipate the danger a minority in a newly seceded state might encounter.

Some Union men thought it best to leave Chattanooga. The manager of the bluff furnace, a New Jersey man, found this the best solution as did J. W. Wilder, accused of being a New York correspondent. Editor James Hood of the *Chattanooga Gazette* found a "self-appointed conclave" determining his fate but got away through the assistance of friends.

Tom Crutchfield had trouble at the Crutchfield House. Volunteer troops using the trains to get to Virginia passed through Chattanooga and expected to be fed at the hotel. Since the Confed-

Missionary Ridge Tunnel. This railroad tunnel, completed in 1858, was the scene of heavy fighting in 1863. Today it is the headquarters of the Tennessee Valley Railroad Museum.

eracy had no arrangements to care for men in transit, Crutchfield lost heavily, for the young recruits either had no money or no intention of paying. The proprietor claimed that he suffered personal abuse as well as financial loss up to $10,000.

Many Hamiltonians stubbornly remained loyal to the United States. Among this group were Wilson Hixson, Levi and D. C. Trewhitt, A. M. and G. O. Cate, A. A. Pearson, William Clift, R. C. McRee, and William Crutchfield. Neighbors who represented the Confederate cause included David M. and Summerfield Key, John L. Hopkins, Peter Turney, Samuel Williams, Robert Hooke, A. M. Johnson, and James A. Whiteside who died in 1860.

Mars' Wrath

William Clift, a well-to-do, tenacious, senior citizen of the Soddy area, went so far as to establish a Union camp at the Sale Creek meeting grounds and initiated a training program for civilian recruits. Confederate authorities decided to break up this defiant sign of Lincolnism. Fortunately, before they fired on each other, a truce was arranged on September 19 called the "Crossroads treaty." All agreed to go home and try to live with their differing opinions. But the terms of the formally written document were soon violated; the Union men reassembled to go on with Clift's War by throwing up earthworks and building a wooden cannon.

Then on November 9 Union civilians throughout east Tennessee, believing they had the support of a Federal army, burned railroad bridges to disrupt Confederate rail travel. Two Hamilton County spans over South Chickamauga Creek were destroyed. The bridge burners actually did little damage, but Union people or those suspected of Union sympathy suffered severely. Many arrests were made and civilians imprisoned. People associated with Clift felt the heavy hand of retaliation.

On November 14 Confederate troops arrived in Chattanooga to deal with the trouble. The next day they were off toward Clift's camp; a mounted Rhea County Home Guard also started out. By mistake the two groups fired on each other, causing the only casualties in Clift's War. Meanwhile the Union men, realizing they were outnumbered, dispersed. Many headed for Kentucky to enlist in the Federal Army.

The Union people of Hamilton County experienced further problems the next year when the Confederacy passed its conscription legislation. Some men, caught in the draft, served only until they could desert, while additional civilians slipped away to Kentucky to join blue-clad comrades.

The county's war record in 1862 took on many unexpected forms. With the fall of Nashville refugees fleeing by train crowded the local depot and hotels awaiting connections. Irregular schedules added to the hysteria as women and children hastened to get away from the fury of war. In addition, between 1000 and 1200 sick and convalescing soldiers from hospitals in the state capital arrived in box and cattle cars unattended by medical personnel. Hamiltonians rallied to provide fuel, cots, covers, bread, and other foodstuffs while converting vacant warehouses into sick bays. No political or military authority guided their efforts and no Confederate funds were available to pay expenses.

Chattanooga had scarcely caught its breath when word circulated about a gang of raiders' capture of a Western and Atlantic train deep in Georgia. When it became known that James Andrews and his men had abandoned the *General* just before reaching Hamilton County, the entire community was aroused. Posses of farmers with dogs and squirrel guns joined the garrison militia in hunting down the 22 men. Eventually all were caught, taken to the Crutchfield House for questioning and imprisoned. Here Andrews received a death sentence, escaped, and was recaptured, keeping the civilians constantly on the alert.

On June 7, 1862, a Union reconnaissance appeared on the north bank of the river after crossing Walden Ridge. Sharpshooters and artillerymen gave the area its first experience under arms; "there was considerable noise & bursting of shells before the blue clad soldiers withdrew." This action was followed by the concentration of all of General Braxton Bragg's men in the Chattanooga area in July in preparation for his invasion of Kentucky. Some 27,000 men eventually poured in; water was scarce; church buildings were commandeered; the Crutchfield House was converted to a hospital; red tape abounded. A quasi-military newspaper, the *Chattanooga Rebel,* published its first edition on August 1, 1862, giving the Hamilton people their first journal in months.

Chickamauga and Chattanooga National Military Park, the oldest and largest military park in the country. The scene is the location of General Braxton Bragg's headquarters on Missionary Ridge.

Almost a year had passed since Bragg led his men across Walden Ridge for the Kentucky campaign prior to his return to Chattanooga, but all this time a garrison force totally submerged the area in military affairs. Occasionally local girls took part in dances, fund-raising parties, and outdoor excursions with the troopers. On August 21, 1863, the quiet enjoyed by the Confederates who were encamped in various parts of the county came to an end. Federal troops under General John T. Wilder appeared in the northern part of the county.

One of Wilder's men wrote: ". . . numbers of Union people came down from the mountain sides, all dressed in their sunday clothes to watch us as we moved by. These people had been hiding in the mts dodging the conscript officers for two years and their greeting that 'we 'uns' mighty glad to see 'youens' told more in the expression of their faces than their words conveyed."

Wilder's troops made noisy demonstrations along the north bank of the Tennessee to divert Bragg from the main Union advance. They threw shells into Chattanooga toward the depot and Crutchfield House and finally forced the *Rebel* to flee southward. On September 9 they received support from an advance unit of General Thomas L. Crittenden's command; as the Confederates evacuated Chattanooga, the Union troops took charge without any resistance. One soldier noted, "The town has a dirty, dreary appearance, almost deserted of citizens [;] very few nice houses and all old ones."

Most of the soldiers moved on to fight at Chickamauga. Since the Federal command made no provision for the kind of reverses they suffered on that field, their defeat resulted in entrapment and siege in Chattanooga. Foraging parties from both armies had already swept rural Hamilton County of any surplus food, poultry, and farm animals, leaving the people in a serious condition. In Chattanooga civilians "were forced to huddle together in the middle of town as best they could . . . ."

The Federal troops bordered on starvation. Only one route to their base of supply at Bridgeport, Alabama, some 60 miles away was open. Teams struggled in the October rains to pull wagons with food, medicine, forage, and ammunition over the Anderson Pike, across Walden Ridge, and down the east side over the W Road. By the end of October, however, a new "cracker line" using the Tennessee River to Kelly's Ferry relieved the situation after the night battle at Wauhatchie on the 28th and 29th of the month assured control of the way into Chattanooga. Meanwhile the army threw up breastworks everywhere in town and placed cannon on every elevation. The trees were all felled, fences disappeared, and streets deteriorated. Hurriedly the government assembled a powerful military command: Generals Blair, Grant, Hooker, Howard, Sheridan, Sherman, Slocum, "Baldy" Smith, and Thomas.

The operation they launched to break out of the siege was thoroughly planned and well executed. It was made spectacular by the extent of the lines and the nature of the terrain. General Bragg wrote to his wife about the unusual scene from Missionary Ridge: "Just underneath my HD Qtrs. are the lines of the two armies, and beyond with their outposts and signal stations are Lookout, Raccoon, and Walden mountains. At night all are brilliantly lit up in the most gorgeous manner by the miriads of camp fires. No scene in the most splended theater ever approached it."

The Union victories at Lookout Mountain and Missionary Ridge jarred open the southern gateway and strategy called for the transformation of the area immediately from a besieged place into a huge forward base for a campaign against Atlanta. The railroads were made a part of the United States Military Railroad system; busy sawmills in every part of the county devoured the forests. The military built a shipyard, reservoir, great warehouses, wagon yards, artillery parks, corrals, a rolling mill, hospitals, and a bridge across the Tennessee River. They continued to use hotels, churches, and homes for offices, hospitals, ordnance depots, and prisons. The Baptist Church served as the Post Chapel. Sutlers' shops and tents lined the streets doing business with military personnel and civilians. For a time the government imposed a program of price control on all merchandise to restrain inflation and waged a war on black market activities.

Traders, camp followers, soldiers, refugees, and freedmen overwhelmed the small remnant of the old population of Chattanooga. Across the river a special site for freedmen, called Camp

Civil War fortifications at Tyner, built by the Confederates to protect the railroad.

Contraband, counted as many as 3500 temporary residents. The provost marshal ran civilian affairs and it was not until October 7, 1865, that a civilian city government was elected.

With war's end, demobilization came fast and by April of 1866 uniforms had disappeared. Tons of ammunition were shipped away; piles of scrap metal collected for reworking. Supplies of every description were auctioned to individual buyers. By September of 1865 the railroads were returned to former owners; the rolling mill was leased, the reservoir sold, and the bridge given to Chattanooga.

Hamilton County had experienced more and suffered more from the war years than most local areas. Trees had been ruthlessly cut, the scars of field works blemished hillsides, and the hastily-built warehouses were credits to no architect. Rural Hamilton County had the appearance of a neglected and weary frontier place.

As the physical landscape sustained loss, so did the spirit of the citizens. The *Chattanooga Gazette,* revived by editor Hood with the protection of the army, was replete with announcements of sheriff sales. Bushwhackers ran rampant; some fought with persons of opposite views while others took advantage of the chaotic times for personal gain. Ooltewah, Tyner, Harrison, Bonny Oaks, and other places harbored bands of these desperadoes.

New Beginnings

The census of 1870 reported a population of 17,241, about 4000 more than a decade earlier, and war had left government and politics on all levels in a state of unpredictable flux. As early as March of 1864 Hamilton County held an election, the first in three years. While it failed to get the popular support the military governor hoped for, it did give the county a set of elected officials. Only 75 persons voted: the winning sheriff got only 29 votes.

In November at least some polls again opened and, although there appears to be no official record of results, some Hamiltonians voted in the presidential election for the Lincoln-Johnson ticket. Their votes, however, did not count, for the electoral college refused to consider ballots from the Volunteer State, maintaining that Tennessee was out of the Union.

Early in 1865 eligible voters had a chance to take part in state elections. They approved an amendment abolishing slavery and elected a civilian governor. The victor, Radical William G. Brownlow, ran without opposition and got all of Hamilton County's 705 votes. Brownlow's Reconstruction regime was over by 1870 as Conservatives rapidly chipped away his power and in that year a new state constitution was prepared, featuring universal manhood suffrage and a poll tax. Hamilton and some adjoining counties were represented in the convention by David M. Key, Democrat and ex-Confederate officer.

On the whole, Hamilton County escaped humiliating effects of the Radical era. The county along with Chattanooga did become a metropolitan police district in which state authorities appointed the local police, who were to be paid by the local people. This ploy infuriated Hamiltonians, for it created political patronage and put unusual power in the hands of the governor. Hamilton County refused to have anything to do with it; Chattanooga fought it through injunctions and court decisions until the state supreme court upheld the law, leaving the city with an $18,000 debt.

Topside, a landmark of Summertown on Signal Mountain, built in 1883 by Judge D. M. Key. Key was the first ex-Confederate officer to serve in the

More important locally was a major issue settled by referendum on June 24, 1870. At that time "that swollen village" Chattanooga was the county's economic and political hub, and the issue arose as to whether it should also be the county seat. The voters agreed that it should be, and on December 5, 1870, the last court convened at Harrison. In Chattanooga the records and offices occupied used buildings until 1879 when the eminence on which the present courthouse stands was acquired and an imposing brick structure erected. This building served until destroyed in 1910 when struck by lightning; the present courthouse was completed three years later.

The relocation of the county seat did not please everyone. Folks in the eastern section fumed, and finally they managed to get a law passed creating a new county on January 30, 1871. This measure incorporated a large portion of Hamilton County and a slice of Bradley into James County. It actually reduced the size of Hamilton by about one-third.

Immediately a new argument arose in "Jim" County over the location of the county seat, and Harrison lost to the village of Ooltewah. The rural James County struggled over finances until 1919 when, in bankrupt condition, the state approved its abolition. A second referendum—953 for and 78 against—merged James into Hamilton County, which in turn absorbed the former's indebtedness. This is the only time Tennessee gave up a county and only very rarely has a county disappeared from any of the states in the country.

Postwar local elections were close, bi-partisan contests with the Republicans generally victorious. Not until 1892 did both the county and Chattanooga give the Democrats a victory, and to celebrate it they had to borrow Republican equipment. In Chattanooga the first postwar mayors were old residents who had supported the Union, but after 1869 newcomers, General John T. Wilder, for example, carried the moderate Republican banner to victory. In 1874 Dr. Philander Sims became the first postwar Democratic mayor who had served the Confederacy.

The blacks, largely concentrated in Chattanooga, generally supported the Republican party. In the city they gained not only the right to vote but the right to hold office by 1868. That year C. P.

James County Courthouse in Ooltewah. James County (1871-1919) was the only Tennessee county to consolidate with another. The courthouse, built in 1913, has been used for many community purposes since that time.

Letcher won a seat on the Board of Aldermen. Numerous others later served in this capacity, including Charles Grigsby and Hiram Tyree. Blacks won many minor offices and various patronage jobs with the fire companies, police force, and board of education. In 1881 seven blacks worked on a 12-man police force.

The first black to occupy a county office was John James Irvine, who was elected circuit court clerk in 1886. In the 1880s the area sent two blacks to the Legislature, William C. Hodge and Styles L. Hutchins. They were two of 12 blacks to sit in the General Assembly in that period; nine came from West Tennessee and one from Davidson County. The era of Negro officeholding on the state level came to an end in 1887 until conditions changed in 1965. In Chattanooga it ended with the emergence of Jim Crow laws throughout the South and particularly with the adoption of the mayor-commission form of government in 1911 which featured all citywide election contests.

Reunion

At the close of the war or soon after, young men who had served in one or the other of the armies moved to Hamilton County. These newcomers were made up of a considerable number of Union veterans who had campaigned in the area along with others from the North who had learned of its potential. Xenophon Wheeler, a Yale graduate, for example, thought if the region was so strategically important in war, then it should be an important business location in peacetime. Some of the prominent Yankees included: T. J. Carlisle, Hiram Chamberlain, H. Clay Evans, Jack Gahagan, J. F. Loomis, J. E. MacGowan, Theodore Montague, John B. Nicklin, Z. C. Patten, T. H. Payne, W. P. Rathburn, Theodore Richmond, T. R. Stanley, S. Bartow Strang, J. H. Van Deman, G. W. Wheland, John T. Wilder, and Henry D. Wyatt.

A number of these men married into local ex-Confederate families: Z. C. Patten to Dora Hagan, John B. Nicklin to Lizzie Kaylor, W. J. Colburn and P. J. Cleary to the daughter and the widow of prewar Congressman R. B. Brabson, and S. B. Moe to Katie Parham. Others formed business partnerships with veterans

First Baptist Church, one of the oldest black congregations in Chattanooga. The building, begun in 1885, is a landmark of the traditional black community.

who had worn the gray: one law firm so composed started practice even before Appomattox.

Relations between these newcomers and former residents who returned or southerners who moved in were strengthened by the community service of two ministers. The Reverend T. H. McCallie, who had stayed in town during the entire contest, and the Reverend Jonathan W. Bachman, who knew the agony of the lost cause, preached faith and harmony.

At first there were a few strident voices calling for retribution of the defeated southland, but they fast disappeared. Some social differences did exist between persons of southern and northern backgrounds, but the new citizens displayed no tendency toward political adventurism; instead, they focused on the future, not the past, through a balanced economy.

Serious adversity also drew the people together in a common concern for the region. The Tennessee River flood of 1867, the greatest recorded flood, swept away bridges, mills, homes, all waterfront structures, and livestock; a steamboat even journeyed down Market Street. Numerous major fires like the one that destroyed the Crutchfield House helped inspire a deep spirit of neighborliness. The late summer epidemic of yellow fever which took 366 lives, forcing hundreds to flee to the countryside and totally disrupting business, demanded social cooperation.

Two men in particular helped direct the early course along the road to reunion: D. M. Key and William Crutchfield. Key, a young lawyer, moved to Chattanooga in 1852. He was one of the political leaders who invited Jefferson Davis to speak at the local hotel in 1861. During the war Key found refuge for his family away from Chattanooga while he served in the military, rising to the rank of lieutenant colonel. At the end of the war Key sought the advice of William Crutchfield about coming back home; he was told that his family would not only be treated well but also that former residents gladly would help old friends.

Key returned in 1865 and renewed his law practice. Five years later he served the area as a delegate to the state constitutional convention and received the appointment as chancellor. In 1872 Key ran for Congress as an Independent Democrat, insisting that the idea of a solid south was unsound and that the color line be

St. Peter and Paul's Catholic Church. This Gothic structure was begun
in 1888 on a site which had long been the center of Catholic activity.

Tucker Baptist Church, McCallie Avenue and Park Street. Built in 1899 with R. H. Hunt as architect for the Trinity M. E. Church, it is of modified Gothic design.

removed from politics. His opponent, Republican William Crutch-field, had mellowed considerably and had no desire to retaliate against former foes. Crutchfield won by a narrow margin, 9950 to 8921. Key in 1875 received an appointment to the U.S. Senate upon the death of the incumbent, Andrew Johnson, and delivered the eulogy for the former president before the Senate. Both Key and Crutchfield were ready to forget the past.

General Wilder, too, understood what was happening. In 1871 he won the mayoralty election but resigned before the end of his term; the mayor *pro tem* who succeeded him had been a Confederate veteran. Wilder as iron manufacturer and vigorous promoter of East Tennessee wrote, "This [Chattanooga] is the freest town on the map. All join together here for the general good and strive to a man for the upbuilding of the city."

To celebrate the nation's centennial, local veterans of the two armies worked together harmoniously. The press noted this spirit in calling attention to "the perfect harmony." It was a year later, however, when the reunion idea was displayed most dramatically. On Decoration Day (May 10) the Confederate Memorial Association laid the cornerstone of the Confederate monument at the cemetery. Local Union veterans participated.

The next day Confederate veterans met to plan a return of the courtesy. They requested the privilege of taking part in the Memorial Day (May 30) exercises at the national cemetery to show "the people of the United States that we cherish none of the bad feelings engendered by the late war. . . ." Without uniforms, banners, or badges and according to the *Chattanooga Times* editorial with "no room for hypocrisy," that Memorial Day service placed the region fully on the road to reunion.

This spirit, then, was caught up in the national spotlight. In the compromise settlement of the disputed presidential election of 1876 Rutherford Hayes agreed to place a Southerner in the national cabinet. He turned to David Key to be postmaster general— the first Southerner, first Democrat, and first Confederate officer to receive such a postwar appointment. To dispel Southern doubts, the newly-elected president toured Dixie. In Chattanooga he was greeted by an editorial that concluded: "We ask you to give us your hands in this matter in all sincerity, that the early days of a united brotherhood may break once more and all hearts rejoice that the night has passed forever."

The New South

This general tendency to look to the future was in accord with the economic spirit of the time. In Hamilton County and the surrounding region, coal and iron were spoken about with an almost religious fervor; transporation by river and rail was not far behind. Immediately after the war the Sale Creek and Soddy coal

mines reopened with Welsh miners sending their fuel to market by
the river. Two Union soldiers activated the iron industry: John T.
Wilder and Hiram Chamberlain incorporated the Roane Iron
Company at Rockwood in 1867 and acquired the old government
rolling mill in Chattanooga three years later. In the following years
the Chattanooga Furnace and the Citico Furnace came into blast.

The chief economic topic of the day turned on the iron industry; prospectors and investors sent out agents to scour the hillsides
for mining and furnace sites. Foreign and domestic investors got
hearty welcomes. However, it was found that the local ores created
serious problems when it came to making steel. For 25 years
management struggled with the latest technology before recognizing defeat. The local ore was in veins too thin to be exploited
gainfully and contained too much phosphorous to make quality
products. Moreover, competition from the burgeoning steel center
of Birmingham, Alabama, made continuing operations unprofita-
ble. Spin-offs from these efforts in the form of iron fabricating
plants and hollow ware firms, however, continue as active enterprises.

Traffic on the Tennessee River bounced back after hostilities
ceased. Packets, homemade flatboats, and giant rafts delivering
logs to such mills as that of Loomis & Hart jammed the landing at
Chattanooga while the social significance of the return of shipping
was felt all along the river. But the stretches of bad water still
limited expansion. River enthusiasts, with Chattanoogans in the
forefront, called for help from the federal government as early as
1868 despite the recent contest involving states' rights. Seven years
later the United States started work on a New Muscle Shoals Canal
and a wave of unrestrained optimism rippled across the entire
valley. Hamilton County interests invested in new steamboats only
to have all hopes dashed by 1890 by the inadequacies of the
completed waterway.

In these glorious years of the steamboat tradition railroad
backers also demanded expanded facilities. John C. and Daniel N.
Stanton brought vigorous times to Chattanooga. They managed to
secure liberally granted Reconstruction money from the state of
Alabama with which they jerrybuilt the Alabama and Chattanooga
Railroad. At the same time using "carpetbag money" and much

Gaskill House, located at 427 East Fifth Street and constructed around 1883, features a mixture of Italianate and Eastlake architecture.

credit they built a hotel in Chattanooga, the Stanton House, before their bubble burst. Their railroad, in constant financial trouble, was bought in 1877 by the Erlanger Company of London and renamed the Alabama Great Southern. (Baron Erlanger's gift to help build a hospital accounts for the use of his wife's name for the institution.)

The city of Cincinnati planned, financed, and built the second postwar railroad into Hamilton County. This 338-mile line with its many bridges and tunnels was completed on March 17, 1880. It proved especially beneficial to the residents of the northern part of the county, for it provided the first rail transportation in that section. The coal mining interests had new markets opened and the property owners along the right-of-way saw the possibility of new cash crops—strawberries, peaches, berries, grapes, and vegetables. Clusters of new dwellings dotted the land around the rural depots.

Still more railroads were built. The Chattanooga, Rome, and Columbus, begun in 1887, eventually formed a section of the Central of Georgia. In 1891 the Chattanooga Southern initiated operations to Gadsden, Alabama, under the leadership of Charles E. James; in time it became the TAG (Tennessee, Alabama, and Georgia). Charlie James, indefatigable promoter, builder, and developer of his home area, planned a belt line railroad around Chattanooga which practically surrounded the city by 1884, operating both freight and passenger service while stimulating the growth of suburbs.

A Board of Trade, started in 1870, went through a period of expansion from the Iron, Coal, and Manufacturers Association to the broader role of the Chamber of Commerce in 1887 with David B. Loveman as president. These promotional groups took pleasure in advertising the region as a great railroad center. The emergence of trunk lines across America added to their bluster: in 1890 the Nashville, Chattanooga, and St. Louis Railway leased the road to Atlanta, thus creating a major north-south route, and about 1894 the new symbol of the Southern Railway system appeared on at least three local lines.

The railroad age reached its zenith on December 1, 1909, with the dedication of the elaborate Southern terminal station. Although many shippers complained of discriminatory freight rates and turned to river carriers in an effort to get more favorable

Terminal Station (Chattanooga Choo-Choo). In 1909 the Southern Railway completed this grand station. After the end of rail passenger service, it stood as a deserted relic until May 30, 1973, when it reopened as a historical preservation project with formal gardens, shops, hotel and restaurant facilities, and a recreation and convention complex.

terms, the railroads remained the backbone of the transportation system. In 1970 and 1971 all passenger trains were discontinued; the Union depot was razed and the terminal station sealed until reopened on May 30, 1973, as the Chattanooga Choo-Choo, a business restoration project and reminder of yesteryear.

Utilities

The idea of a balanced economy was aided by technological advances and the presence of at least a minimum amount of venture capital. In Chattanooga a gas company opened for limited service in 1870 with two miles of mains. The gas, used chiefly for home lighting, fueled some jets on Market Street which were lit each evening by a fellow on horseback carrying a kind of blowtorch.

On September 4, 1875, the maiden trip of the horse car—drawn by mules—carried passengers from the river along Market Street to Montgomery (Main Street) to the delight of all civic boosters. Some 14 years later a different source of energy propelled the cars; in spite of citizens' fears that exposed electric currents would bring disaster, the electric car made its appearance. Soon a flock of small companies laid track on the main city streets and extended their lines far into the county.

Another innovation started as a kind of plaything which caused skeptics to scoff. In 1878 a telephone line, strung from the Stanton House to a livery stable, speeded service for guests. Two years later an exchange bragged of 52 subscribers. All of them had low numbers with #1 assigned to Tshopik's Garden, the fashionable cake and ice cream parlor. Expansion was slow, and some church groups discussed the moral issue associated with Sunday conversations over the wire. After a decade had passed, about 450 telephones, mostly business instruments, were in operation.

An additional marvel took form on May 6, 1882. Current from a small generator lit a few electric lights used as advertising gimmicks rather than as lanterns to brighten dark places. Loveman's store and the Read House each noted that they had three globes while the *Chattanooga Times* claimed it had the highest light on the street.

The county joined in the parade of progress although with some reluctance on the part of people in the northern section when it contracted in 1889 for the construction of a river bridge. This span, called the "county bridge," came to be known as the Walnut Street bridge and cost almost one quarter of a million dollars. With the exception of the few years when the military bridge stood, the only way to cross the Tennessee River before this structure was finished was by ferry.

A Journalist's Role

Through the postwar years people were short of funds but very long on enthusiasm. This gusto suited the temper of a young newcomer who arrived in Chattanooga in the 1870s. Acquainted with the printing business, he was unshaken in his determination to publish a newspaper. In 1878 Adolph S. Ochs acquired the poverty-ridden *Chattanooga Times* which had been started in 1869. Since Ochs had not reached the age of legal maturity, his father signed the necessary papers completing a deal which gave the youth one-half interest in the firm, including complete control of the paper, for $250 with the option to buy the remaining portion at the end of two years for a negotiated sum.

The new publisher insisted on professionalism in his journal while preaching the doctrine of diversified economy for the South. No one sounded the trumpet of praise for Hamilton County or Chattanooga louder than he; no one had more energy. Ochs was the promoter of every project. Wags claimed that the city could never fail, for it had "an Ochs to pull them along." Except for party politics, he was the mainspring of all civic and cultural activity and a key member of every committee.

When the public grew dissatisfied with the old James Hall "showroom" or theater, the New Opera House Company was organized under Ochs's aegis. A decorously renovated facility (later called the Lyric) opened on October 4, 1886, with great fanfare. For years it represented the cultural center of the county. Here the great Sarah Bernhardt starred along with many other artists and, when the hall was razed in 1913 to make way for commercial progress, it was said that "there is probably no building in all of Chattanooga which is dearer to old residents."

Although Ochs was too young to have served in the Civil War, he took an interest in veterans' affairs. In June of 1888 Henry V.

Boynton, a Federal regimental commander at the battle of Chickamauga, conceived of a plan for preserving the battlefield as a historic laboratory. The next year the Society of the Army of the Cumberland held its reunion in Chattanooga; Ochs served as chairman of the local committee. To further the park idea, Confederate veterans were sent invitations to participate in these arrangements. Plans were expanded, however, and soon it was decided to approach the government as sponsor of this unique scheme.

The National Military Park

The local congressman, H. Clay Evans, carried the bill passed by Congress to create Chickamauga Chattanooga National Military Park to the president for his signature on August 19, 1890. Three commissoners were given the responsibility of acquiring land, marking the field, approving the erection of Federal markers, and supervising state monuments and markers. Boynton became park historian.

The fundamental idea incorporated in the legislation was the preservation of the field as it was at the time of the conflict without any consideration for beautification. Although the major portion of the acreage acquired was in north Georgia, Hamilton County locations encompassed Orchard Knob, Bragg's Missionary Ridge Headquarters, the De Long Reservation, and 45 acres known as Sherman's Reservation. Title to approach roads, Crest Road on Missionary Ridge and Hooker Road from Lookout Mountain to the ridge, was part of the overall plan.

Dedication exercises were held on September 18, 19, and 20, 1895, with Vice-President of the United States Adlai Stevenson as master of ceremonies. Hamilton County and Chattanooga joined in the gala with publisher Ochs again serving as chairman of local planning. Frantic preparations preceded those busy days which brought 74 special trains and numerous steamboats jammed with passengers to Chattanooga: an omen of the millions of visitors to follow. The city in appreciation of the role of Boynton presented him with a large silver service.

It soon became obvious that certain principal battle sites had been omitted from the original purchases. In 1896 some 85 acres

Dome Building. Known also as the Ochs Building, it was constructed in 1891 as the home of the Chattanooga *Times*. Its domed corner bay is a local landmark.

Old Post Office, East 11th Street. This Romanesque building, built in the early 1890s, is used today by the TVA.

on the saddle of Lookout Mountain, including the Cravens House, were added and two years later Ochs with the help of Alexander W. Chambliss spearheaded a drive to acquire 16½ acres at the point of Lookout Mountain for the park. In 1910 the appropriate and splendid New York Peace Monument was dedicated.

Although publisher Ochs had moved away from Chattanooga when he purchased the *New York Times* in 1896, he never lost interest in the area which had given him his start. To prevent crass commercialism from destroying the beauty of Lookout Mountain, he led a campaign to acquire the wild forest lands on the mountainsides. Donations of money and land resulted in a gift to the national government on June 22, 1935, of some 2700 acres to be added to the national park.

In recognition of his long association with the park—the oldest and largest military park in the country—an observatory museum was dedicated to the memory of Adolph S. Ochs at the point of Lookout Mountain on November 12, 1940. It was intended as a tribute not to a warrior who fought there but to a citizen who understood the meaning of the bloody struggle and the strength the conflict brought to a reunited land.

Other essential military areas were later donated to the national park: in 1948 some seven acres at Signal Point on Signal Mountain and in 1977 Sunset Rock on Lookout Mountain. Interestingly, other strategic areas of military importance never became national lands. However, Hamilton County and the city of Chattanooga acquired Moccasin Bend, long discussed as a park site, and jointly set it apart for public usage on June 20, 1961. Cameron Hill, where many a soldier, Confederate and Union, fought, never was made a part of the national park. In 1905 when the friends of Boynton living in Hamilton County learned of his death, they created a reservation on its summit in his name. Although greatly altered since that time, it recognizes the contribution of an adopted son to the heritage of the region.

The Boom

The original planning and development of Chickamauga Chattanooga National Military Park coincided with an incredible real estate and construction boom typical of this part of the South. In Chattanooga town lots attracted buyers as prices rose, and conversation turned to the subject of mortgage terms while store fronts changed into real estate offices. In the surrounding countryside, especially along the route of the belt line railway, promoters drove stakes in old fields to mark off new streets in such subdivisions as Orchard Knob, Highland Park, East Lake, Ridgedale, St. Elmo, and Sherman Heights. The swapping, trading, and buying of property reached into Hill City across the river and onto Walden Ridge where the local newspaper offered subscribers the chance to win a lot in Timesville.

The biggest operation involved the Chattanooga Land, Coal, Iron & Railway Company popularly referred to as the "Over-the-River Company." This speculative company claimed title or options to some 25,000 acres of land between Hill City and Walden Ridge where a dream city was to explode suddenly into a prosperous reality. Such ventures brought some outside money to the area and young citizen recruits like Edward Y. Chapin. Adolph Ochs, deeply committed and finding it necessary to raise funds to meet his obligations, purchased the *New York Times* as a consequence and moved to the East.

Chattanooga Car Barns Complex; urban transportation center
(1887 to 1978); currently used as a sports barn and commercial
retail center.

Real estate investment was accompanied by subdivision home
construction and grandiose commercial schemes. In Chattanooga
promoters prepared an attractive "package" for Cameron Hill. A
horse carline, an incline railway, park, pagoda, big hotel, water
company, and a "first class beer garden and concert hall" comprised parts of a vigorous advertising campaign. By 1890 the
incline, pagoda, garden, and water standpipe showed evidence of
the determined attitude of the builders, but the national depression of 1893 and the failing local economy caused a complete
collapse of the bubble within seven years.

The eternal lure of the river also attracted investment funds. In
the last great days of the steamboat era John A. Patten, president of
three packet lines and the Tennessee River Improvement Association, was the local guiding spirit along with Captain Walter C.
Wilkey, one of the river's most popular skippers. Commodious
packets—the *Gunter, Joe Wheeler, Chattanooga, Avalon,* and *John A.
Patten*—gave a special luster to the old Tennessee River in the
declining years of its commercial and passenger business.

Much more attractive to the promoter and more bizarre in
execution were the undertakings on Lookout Mountain. Summer
hotel service was resumed shortly after peace came in 1865. At this

Lookout Mountain Incline Railway, constructed in 1895 and in service
ever since. Called the "World's Most Amazing Mile," it reaches a grade
of 72.7 percent.

time the prime mountain property, Point Lookout, was owned and managed by Harriet Straw Whiteside, widow of the early booster of the area, James A. Whiteside. In 1879 a stock company built a second turnpike up Lookout to compete with the original Whiteside road. A "turnpike war" followed; Mrs. Whiteside sold monopolistic privilege to a livery stable to use her road to take visitors to the mountain and exclusive entrance to the Point. Spirited lawsuits ensued, leading to a decision allowing anyone who paid the admission fee to enter the area. The owner countered by closing the Point to all comers.

A new phase in the commercial rivalry emerged. In March of 1888 the Lookout Incline Railway Company operated its first cars on Incline #1 from St. Elmo to a large hotel located at the foot of the palisades under the Point. From spacious balconies extending around three sides of the inn guests enjoyed the same panoramic view as seen from the Point. A narrow gauge railroad, built on the "brink of space," ran along the base of the bluffs to Sunset Rock. The breathtaking location brought hotel guests from all parts of the country while the prospects of increased tourism generated by the national military park spurred on a new wave of competition.

Before Incline #1 began regular service, another group of entrepreneurs undertook the construction of a broad gauge railroad over which freight and Pullman cars could be brought to the summit of the mountain without any transfer in town. This company also hoped to benefit from a large land sale of property they owned adjacent to the Whiteside holdings. In addition, they built a huge 365-room hotel named the Lookout Inn which welcomed its first guests in June of 1890. The railroad never shook off serious financial problems, and the hotel periodically closed and opened until destroyed by fire on November 17, 1908.

Despite ephemeral profits, other investors and builders joined in the task of conquering the mountain. A charter dated June 1, 1895, brought Incline #2 into legal existence. (This is the present incline now operated by CARTA and advertised as "America's Most Amazing Mile." Lookout Inn stood across the highway from the mountain incline station.)

The "turnpike war" gave way to new technology. The continuing contest for control now involved two inclines, two hotels, and

Hutcheson House, 360 South Crest Road, Missionary Ridge, built in 1894 in the grand manner of the late Victorian style.

broad and narrow gauge railways with the Whiteside acres at the Point still the center of the feud. This time, however, alert residents interested the national government in acquiring the historic land for the military park, which removed it for all time from gross commercialism.

Schools

The absorption in material things in the postwar decades left little time for consideration of cultural activities or education. In Chattanooga freedmen's classes and a Post School sponsored by the government attempted to provide training for refugees and some local residents immediately after Appomattox. A few small private schools started, the most important being the co-educational Lookout Mountain Educational Institute which held classes from 1866 to 1872. Housed in old Union army hospital buildings on Lookout Mountain, this "college" enjoyed the financial support of Christopher R. Robert, a New York City philanthropist who wanted to help southern white children. However, after six years he cut off his support because of poor health and a desire to concentrate his resources on strengthening Robert College in Constantinople, Turkey.

During these same years blacks could attend a new school provided in part by the government and the American Missionary Association. The Reverend E. O. Tade, a Negro Congregational Church minister, came to town from Memphis to launch the project, named in honor of General Oliver Otis Howard, soldier and able Freedmen's Bureau commissioner. According to Tade, the school in 1869 had six teachers and some 850 students. In 1867 the Radical Tennessee state government created a tax-supported public school program. Under the provisions of the law, Tade became Hamilton County's first school superintendent although he had little opportunity to set up a program because the Conservatives of the state in 1870 revoked the law.

Following the abolition of the state system, the city of Chattanooga under the leadership of H. Clay Evans passed an ordinance in 1872 creating a city system. A city board of education appointed Henry D. Wyatt, a New Englander who had served in the Union army, as superintendent. Wyatt won the respect of the community as a talented educator and opened the first graded school for whites on January 1, 1873; in December of the next year he started a high school program with 35 pupils. Five girls composed the first graduating class in 1879. The Howard School was incorporated into the system and put into operation its high school curriculum in 1883.

On the state level, a second tax-supported school program got underway in 1873. As in other counties, Hamilton required real dedication to get a system on track even though the law called for only primary grades. Budgets scarcely existed and there was no tradition to support education. Terms were short, teachers untrained and salaries unattractive. In the rural sections travel problems cut into attendance, and throughout the county the schools suffered because law required separate facilities for the races. So one-room, one-teacher, log or frame schools became the pattern except for Chattanooga.

The 1890 census shows the extent of the progress made. That year the county population numbered 53,482 persons with more than one-half residing in Chattanooga. Of the 29,100 living in the city 43 percent were black. There were 164 teachers in Hamilton County (115 white, 49 black); of this total 74 taught in Chattanooga (45 white, 29 black). The total number of pupils was 10,160 (7106 white, 3054 black) of whom 4541 (2578 white, 1963 black) lived in the city.

Not until 1891 did Tennessee provide for secondary education and Hamilton County reacted slowly to the establishment of high schools, as did most other counties. Beginning about 1902 schools of this level were started at Hixson, Sale Creek, Soddy, Tyner, and Ridgedale (later known as Central High School) with Birchwood added to the list shortly thereafter.

Students often walked five or more miles to class. More fortunate ones drove wagons or buggies, pooled rides with neighbors, or traveled by horseback. The schools had barns of a sort to stable mules and horses during the day and at a later date used horse-drawn buses to transport students. Parochial and private schools supplemented the public system. In 1876 some classes at the Notre Dame School were held in the church basement and ten years later when the school dedicated a large modern building, it reported a student body of 250.

Baylor School opened in 1893 under the direction of J. Roy Baylor. The school was incorporated in 1914 and a board of trustees with J. T. Lupton as president became the policy-making body. One year later it moved to a campus on the Tennessee River at the base of Walden Ridge. McCallie School started in 1905 several miles outside of Chattanooga on the slope of Missionary Ridge donated by the Reverend T. H. McCallie. Its organizers, sons of the minister, governed the institution until 1937 when it became nonprofit under the control of a board of trustees. Another private school, Girls Preparatory School, began classwork under the aegis of Grace McCallie, Tommy Payne Duffy, and Eula Lea Jarnagin. After incorporating, GPS moved to a campus along the river in North Chattanooga.

When the Methodist Episcopal Church made known its desire to establish a central university for its southern conferences, Chattanooga successfully bid for the institution. A board of trustees composed of churchmen and local residents opened the Chattanooga University on September 15, 1886. However, high hopes for the institution were dampened by a complex racial problem and, secondly, by competition with another Methodist school at Athens. Three years after its founding, the school was consolidated with the Athens institution as U.S. Grant University, but undergraduate work was not revived in Chattanooga until 1904. Many changes occurred within a few years including a name change to the University of Chattanooga and in 1909 the deeding of all property to a self-perpetuating board of trustees by the Methodist Church.

A second collegiate institute was originally located in James County. Here one Jim Thatcher owned a lime business, but when demand fell off in 1916, he sold his property at "Thatcher's Switch" to the Southern Junior College, which was operated by the Seventh Day Adventist Church. In due time Thatcher's Switch became Collegedale and the school, Southern Missionary College. Shortly after the annexation of James County by Hamilton the student body numbered 250, ranging from elementary pupils through junior college students. The campus embraced some 750 acres which supported a variety of industries and agricultural pursuits. In 1944 the school became a four-year accredited college and by 1978 enrolled approximately 2000 students.

Creative Arts

Just as education got off to a late and faltering start, so did activities in the creative arts. In the early years Thomas Crutchfield, Sr., did establish a reputation as a skilled builder, and several generations later R. H. Hunt won respect as an accomplished architect. James Cameron located in Chattanooga in the 1850s on the encouragement of James A. Whiteside and from his home and studio on the elevation which bears his name worked as the area's only nineteenth century artist.

Numerous residents, collectors and compilers of local historical data, included E. Y. Chapin, Charles D. McGuffey, T. H. McCallie, John P. Long, Louis L. Parham, Lewis Shepherd, Xenophon Wheeler, and Harry M. Wiltse. Francis Lynde moved to the region as an adult and embarked on a literary career; he published articles, short stories, and novels. Alice MacGowan, on the other hand, came with her family to the county as a young person. Her father commanded the First U.S. Colored Artillery when mustered out in Chattanooga and remained as the editor of the *Chattanooga Times*. Miss MacGowan is best known for her books *Judith of the Cumberlands* and *The Sword in the Mountains*, a Civil War story set in Hamilton County.

The most talented of the writers, Emma Bell Miles, was born in 1879 and brought to the county when nine years of age. She lived near or on Walden Ridge where frontier conditions met the lifestyle of city summer residents. Ever alert to the wonders of nature and the freedom and beauty of the mountains, she found expression for her emotions in splendid little art sketches, poems, and stories. In 1904 she published a sympathetic evaluation of life in the southern highlands under the title, *The Spirit of the Mountains*. This perceptive interpretation stands today as one of the foremost explanations of a basic American way of life. Other of her works are *Our Southern Birds* and *Strains From a Dulcimer*, a volume of poems published posthumously.

Frances Willard Building in Chattanooga

In the field of music a gifted violinist from Prague, Bohemia, assumed leadership following a local engagement in 1893. Joseph Cadek, performer, teacher, and promoter of musical entertainment, founded the Cadek Conservatory in 1904 which became his legacy to the region along with very talented progeny.

Two young blacks, raised in poverty, resided in Chattanooga until their innate artistic abilities found opportunity which won them national and international acclaim. Bessie Smith, born about 1898, earned distinction as one of the truly great blues singers. She performed from Beale Street to Broadway and was probably the first black artist to make phonograph records; Columbia Records designated her "Empress of the Blues."

Roland Hayes, who accompanied his mother to Chattanooga at the age of 15, sang at his work in an iron foundry and at his church before supporters encouraged him to seek training. He joined the famed Fisk Jubilee Singers and later appeared in Europe as a lyric tenor specializing in Afro-American spirituals and German lieder. Hayes sang for royalty at Buckingham Palace and integrated the European concert stage before returning to America where he performed with all the great symphony orchestras. In 1968 the University of Chattanooga awarded him an honorary degree as had his alma mater, Fisk University, for his music and his work in human relations.

Spanish—American War

In 1898 the military returned to Hamilton County to prepare for the Spanish—American War. Because of local facilities and the availability of land at the military park, the government created Camp George H. Thomas (named for the "Rock of Chickamauga"). Although located in neighboring North Georgia, this installation was directly oriented toward Chattanooga. During the summer months more than 72,000 men trained there, often without weapons or uniforms, and lived in barracks hastily built without care for comfort or sanitation.

Typhoid fever broke out at the camp; doctors and nurses could not cope with the epidemic. A total of 450 men died—more than the number killed in action in the war—and thousands more were stricken. The people of Hamilton County spontaneously rallied to render assistance; some opened their homes to sick men; some manned small hospitals sponsored by civic and fraternal groups, while other volunteers traveled to the camp to help convalescents.

The war ended as quickly as it had begun, and by mid-September only a few troops remained at the camp. Although some people complained that the fever was caused by conditions at the site of the training center, others insisted that the area had nothing to do with the cause of the epidemic and worked to get a permanent military installation established. In December of 1904 their goal was accomplished when Fort Oglethorpe was officially opened adjacent to the Chickamauga Chattanooga National Military Park lands in north Georgia.

Enter Jim Crow

A frontier environment lasted long in Hamilton County and the traits of character it nurtured in the people emphasized independence of mind, self-reliance, explosive passion, and suspicion of the law. Violence frequently erupted, leading to tragedy. In 1881, for example, both the sheriff and his deputy were felled in cold blood when two Taylor brothers freed a convicted third member of the family. Such blatant acts also helped to complicate

Second Presbyterian Church. Located at Pine and
West Seventh streets, this structure is a fine exam-
ple of the ecclesiastical design of architect R. H.
Hunt.

Chattanooga Municipal Building, designed by R. H. Hunt and constructed in 1908.

relations between the races although the record for the county was not as excessive as in many parts of the South.

In Chattanooga a sense of community had emerged which provided a climate more favorable for black participation in political affairs. An environment supporting paternalistic racial attitudes developed and a two-party system functioned in which the large percentage of blacks to the total electorate carried weight. In the years following 1865 no hard and rigid legal system of segregation existed except in the field of education. Custom and prejudice set the pattern for white-black relationship. Economic interests in addition contributed to the black acceptance of a "debt of gratitude" approach, for many showed an inclination to accommodate themselves silently to the developments of the day.

Around 1890 certain changes took place in the county which reflected widespread Southern efforts to legalize segregation through Jim Crow laws. With these changes came more talk about "Lily Whites" and "Lamp Blacks" and a growing fear of Negro crime. Although local reaction was not as intense as in many other places, it did introduce a hardening attitude between the races.

The segregation law relating to public transportation drew special attention. A local black woman, Georgia Edwards, took a suit to the Interstate Commerce Commission: she was forced to use second-class accommodations (although she held a first-class ticket) because the railroad had no first-class "separate" accommodations. She won the decision, which brought her some personal recognition but did not materially change travel conditions.

In 1905 Tennessee extended segregation to streetcars; opposition mounted across the state, for such segregation easily led to personal embarrassment. Chattanooga blacks launched a boycott claiming that the law was "an insult to the Negro race." Although many of the black leaders did not speak out on this issue, Randolph M. Miller, the jaunty and provocative editor of the Negro newspaper, *The Blade,* made it a popular issue.

To further the boycott, Miller and his associates organized hack lines to take people to work. Then they tried to charter and organize a bus company. Their plans failed for lack of money and because people believed the organizers were more interested in the bus business than they were in the boycott. The city humane officer put an end to the hack line by threatening to prosecute the operators for "working old worn-out animals from early morning until late at night . . . only half feeding them."

Some sweeping charges were made against the white population because of this episode which the past community record actually did not support. In 1892, for example, the sheriff and his men went far beyond the call of duty in protecting a black charged with assaulting a white woman. They spirited him away from a mob, escorted him to numerous jails across the state, and at one point jumped off a moving train with him to elude a mob at the next station. They risked their positions and their lives in this dangerous journey. Meanwhile, because a hostile uneasiness hung over Chattanooga, citizens called a public meeting with the Reverend T. H. McCallie as chairman. It attracted some 1000 people who wanted to "reverse the apparent order of the day by putting the law above the wild and wooly mob."

Tennessee saluted Hamilton County and her officials for their positive desire and bold efforts to live in peace within the law. These hopes, however, were dashed: in 1893 a mob lynched Alfred Blount, a black; in 1894 a Soddy crowd lynched a black youth, Charles Brown, and on March 19, 1906, Ed Johnson was lynched on the Walnut Street Bridge.

The Johnson case brought unwelcome notoriety to the area. Accused of assaulting a white woman, Johnson was taken out of the county prior to his trial for fear of mob violence. He was slipped into town, tried, found guilty, and sentenced to be executed on March 13. Two black attorneys—Noah W. Parden and Styles L. Hutchins, a former state legislator—appealed the decision in the state supreme court and then in the federal courts. The latter application like the one presented to the Tennessee court was denied, but the judge granted a stay of execution of ten days to allow time for an appeal to the United States Supreme Court.

Emotions ran high; the prisoner was baptized in a prison bath tub. No one really believed Parden and Hutchins could get a hearing in Washington, but they did, and on March 19 a justice ordered a stay of execution pending action by the full court. County officials received this word with an order that Johnson be held in the custody of the local officials pending this appeal. That night an angry mob lynched Johnson. No special precautions had been taken to protect the prisoner, and the newspaper headline the next morning read, "Mandate of the Supreme Court of the United States Disregarded and Red Riot Rampant."

Rumors spread of a Negro uprising; armed guards patroled the streets. Federal justice department investigators arrived to compile evidence of what had occurred, and eventually 28 men were cited in contempt of the Supreme Court. Time passed; in May of 1908 charges were dismissed on all but six. They were found guilty and sentenced November 15, 1909, in a five to three decision of the court. Four were found guilty of taking part in the lynching; the other two, Sheriff Joseph Shipp and Jailor Jeremiah Gibson, were guilty of contempt as a consequence of negligence in not protecting Johnson. The sheriff of Hamilton County and his jailor, both Confederate veterans, were imprisoned in Washington in what is possibly the only case of its nature in our national history.

During the years, continuing efforts were made by some Chattanoogans to reduce the possibility of black success at the polls. Attempts were made to revoke the city charter, to restrict voting privileges, to adopt a secret ballot in the hope of screening out those who could not read, and to eliminate ward voting districts. In 1911 this goal was achieved as a part of a general reform movement when a city mayor-commission form of government was adopted. Since all elections were on a city-wide basis, the chance of a black gaining victory was practically impossible until the 1960s.

The Twentieth Century

In the twentieth century the population of the county steadily mounted while Chattanooga's growth was sporadic and uneven, mainly attributable to the annexation of additional territory:

	Hamilton County		
	Total	Whites	Blacks
1900	61,695	42,187	19,490
1920	115,954	88,829	27,120
1940	180,478	140,845	39,633
1970	254,236	207,236	46,397

	Chattanooga		
	Total	Whites	Blacks
1900	30,154	17,032	13,122
1920	57,895	39,001	18,894
1940	128,163	91,712	36,404
1970	119,082	76,216	42,610

Until the twentieth century the corporate limits of Chattanooga extended from the winding Tennessee River to East End Avenue (now Central Avenue) on the east and to 28th Street close to Chattanooga Creek on the south. Before the real estate boom in the 1880s the stretch of land eastward to Missionary Ridge and southward to the foot of Lookout Mountain remained a wooded area. With the belt line and electric cars a number of satellite villages grew which became the object of annexation starting with Highland Park and Orchard Knob in 1905. In 1913 an estimated 10,000 Hamiltonians found themselves new citizens of Chattanooga when Orange Grove, Ferger Place, Oak Grove Park, and Ridgedale were annexed. Sponsors of annexation mounted a major effort to extend the city in the 1920s leading to the incorporation of East Chattanooga (variously referred to as Amnicola, Tunnel, Sherman Heights, Avondale, and Boyce), Bushtown and Churchville, two black hamlets, and East Lake with its neighbors Cedar Hill and Fort Cheatham. The intensive campaign ended on September 30, 1929, in a big community celebration marking the addition of Alton Park, Brainerd, Missionary Ridge, North Chattanooga, Riverview, and St. Elmo.

Each of these areas had its own story, but the most unusual suburban situation was that of Missionary Ridge, a strictly residential area which incorporated in 1925 and was 4½ miles long and only 1100 feet wide; its width was divided by the Crest Road, owned and maintained by the federal government as part of the national military park.

Busy Years

Most employed workers were associated with small establishments; in 1900 the county reported 332 manufacturing concerns with a total capitalization of something more than $8,000,000. The principal fields included lumber; iron, ores, clay, and building stone; coal and coke; and leather. About 1880 some workers became associated with union movements which for years were organized as "secret societies." In 1897 the American Federation of Labor chartered the local Central Labor Union. Occasional violence flared up with efforts to unionize, the most serious of which was a series of strikes by streetcar employees in 1916 and 1917 which led to several deaths and the use of federal troops from Fort Oglethorpe. Since that time, union organizations have been continually strengthened throughout the county.

When the iron and steel business proved to be an unsatisfactory base for the region's economy, a trend toward diversification got under way. Several entirely new fields formed the groundwork for modern developments. The textile industry, always comparatively small, expanded rapidly under the leadership of John L. Hutchinson, Garnett Andrews, Jr., and Edward Guild Richmond.

A second area, the insurance business, got a start in 1887 when the Provident Life and Accident Company was organized. Its scope rapidly broadened from regional to national coverage under the direction of Thomas Maclellan, a Scot from New Brunswick, Canada, who joined the young firm in 1892. In 1903 a second major company organized as the Volunteer State Life Insurance Company; Z. C. Patten's two-score years as head of this company saw it prosper as an expanding home office. On August 16, 1909, a charter granted the Interstate Life and Accident Insurance Company the right to do business. Hugh D. Huffaker and Dr. Joseph W. Johnson piloted this organization through its early years.

The third newcomer announced its start in an advertisement on November 12, 1899: "Drink a bottle of Coca-Cola. . . ." Ben F. Thomas and Joseph B. Whitehead, soon joined by John Thomas Lupton, had acquired the right to bottle this carbonated beverage from its Atlanta owner, Asa G. Candler. It was an arrangement which proved to be the foundation of a world-wide enterprise.

The three young businessmen divided the United States into two territories: Thomas received the populous east and Whitehead and Lupton controlled bottling rights in the vast remaining area. They adopted a common operating structure: a franchise system

James Building, 735 Broad Street; constructed by Charles E. James, local promoter and developer, and known as Chattanooga's "first skyscraper."

Fort Wood Historic District. Named for an important Civil War redoubt, this district, including some 120 buildings, reflects the building trends from 1880 to 1920.

for the bottling and distribution of the beverage generally using individuals from the area to establish and operate plants. Slow growth was overcome by imaginative marketing promotion, including the creation of the easily recognized "hobble-skirt" bottle. Locally, Coca-Cola had far-reaching importance. Not only did Hamiltonians acquire franchises, but the makers of glass bottles, of wooden beverage cases, and of coolers of a variety of designs enjoyed a neighborly relationship with the bottlers. From the success of this industry have developed several wealthy foundations which have been major benefactors of the region's cultural, educational, and health science services.

Something else was new—all across America men discussed a new source of electric energy. The use of river currents for power blended with the old desire to improve navigation and had the support of John A. Patten's Tennessee River Improvement Association. It also caught the attention of the local congressman, John A. Moon, who served from 1897 to 1921. Moon believed in the systematic improvement of the entire Tennessee River system, but he also believed hydro sites should not be granted to individuals or companies for private profit but should be awarded for the benefit of society. He especially stressed municipal development.

In 1902 Moon introduced legislation for the construction of a dam in Marion County to harness the energy of the "valley of the whirlpool rapids." The structure would be paid for by the recipient of the 99-year power franchise, the locks by the government which also held title to the dam. Chattanooga received the option to the generating rights in the legislation that became law in 1904. The city turned down the offer and, according to the act, the option went to private developers. It passed into the possession of Charles E. James, Chattanooga's promoter and financier, and Josephus C. Guild, engineer and supporter of the electrical business.

With New York financial backing, they organized the Chattanooga and Tennessee River Power Company in 1905 and began construction of the Hales Bar Lock and Dam. One discouragement followed another. Guild died and his son Jo Conn took his place. The dam built over limestone caverns leaked and several engineering companies failed, but finally, on November 13, 1913, it was completed. Chattanooga, which was to get all of the electricity generated, celebrated although a rival company was already furnishing power from the flume along the Ocoee River into Hamilton County. Everyone cheered "the dynamo of Dixie." In 1922 the two companies merged as the Tennessee Electric Power Company. Only one year later the demand for current required the building of a steam plant at Hales Bar.

The year that work started on the dam the Chattanooga Automobile Company advertised as the "only garage" in the area. The fact that the Wallace Buggy Company was a sales agency for Maxwells and other cars shows what was taking place. An estimate for 1909 claimed that 350 motor cars were owned in the county. This happened to be a banner year locally for the horseless carriage. On April 22 one of the biggest sporting events in Hamilton's history attracted huge crowds: a widely advertised race up the 4.9 miles of winding road to the top of Lookout Mountain involving danger, speed, skill, and nationally-known drivers. Some curves sported such names as Moccasin Bend, Spine Scratcher, and Undertaker's Delight. Louis Chevrolet, the dapper Frenchman, ran the record time of six minutes, 30 and 2/5 seconds, but his effort was declared unofficial because he had to make a number of starts to get past the first mile.

The race stimulated interest in cars and roads. By 1920 a truck served as a bus to Soddy High School, the mail service was motorized, and the last police horse in Chattanooga went to permanent pasture. Six years earlier enthusiasts started an automobile club to promote improved roads and the next year the Dixie Highway Association in which Judge M. M. Allison became a leader was organized for the purpose of getting a major north-south highway connecting Detroit and Miami. While Hamiltonians played a key role in this national effort, local improvements also demanded their attention. A tunnel through Stringer's Ridge, built by prison labor without a tunnel engineer, opened a door for the north end of the county (1910) and another, the McCallie Avenue tunnel (1913), eased the way to the east. (The Bachman and Wilcox tubes through Missionary Ridge were started in 1917 and 1930.) In November of 1917 a second Tennessee River bridge, now known as the John Ross Bridge, opened.

The expanding economy welcomed a second major newspaper

when the *Evening News* put its first edition on the street on July 1, 1888. Jerome B. Pound, the young publisher, braved many lean years but got out his journal regularly until 1909 when he sold out to George Fort Milton and associates.

Banking service likewise expanded. An informal clearing house with T. G. Montague as president organized in 1890. In 1905 Thomas Ross Preston launched the Hamilton National Bank which moved six years later into a 15-story building at 7th and Market streets. The American Trust & Banking Company under the guidance of Harry Scott Probasco was started in 1912. Four years later a Morris Plan Bank which later became Pioneer Bank began service with Gaston C. Raoul and later George M. Clark taking the lead in this enterprise.

World War I

The economic spirit of the early twentieth century was interrupted and modified by World War I. When Congress declared war, local whistles and church bells sounded their approval. Some few Hamiltonians already had joined foreign forces; others soon volunteered for special duty, but most of the approximately 10,000 men who served were inducted under the selective service law. Of this number about 200 lost their lives, while the government singled out at least 13 Hamiltonians for special recognition and allied countries cited five, including four who received the French Croix de Guerre.

Echoing the national sentiment, a great hysterical outpouring of loyalty and passionate patriotism marked the war years. Gasless Sundays, heatless Mondays, and meatless days got faithful support. Throughout the county victory gardens occupied hundreds of summer hours; 40 rural and 14 suburban groups organized in processing foodstuffs for home use or sale for the benefit of the Red Cross. Such positive efforts were marred by excessive zeal in other endeavors. Volunteers selling bonds used shame, humiliation, and blatant pressure to meet their quotas in those cases where citizens seemed to be wanting in patriotism. Others clamored loudly to have German studies suspended or to have persons with foreign accents investigated about their loyalty.

The proximity of the county to the training center at Fort

Oglethorpe added another dimension to the war effort. The first sign of this was a gigantic emergency construction program in 1917 involving local suppliers, contractors, and workers while attracting many itinerants. Later medical and sanitary units, called Camp Greenleaf, used University of Chattanooga and Central High School facilities in their training programs. Soldiers filled the shops, hotels, and amusement centers in Chattanooga; the city fathers obligingly made a concession to them by granting movie theaters the right to have Sunday shows.

Virtually every able-bodied person in the county was mobilized for some phase of volunteer work to assist the "boys." They offered travelers' aid, entertainment, and solace. Hostess houses and home entertainment helped reduce the plague of homesickness, while hospital workers aided the medics. During the influenza epidemic in 1918 volunteer work recalled the frantic days of the Spanish–American War fever.

Peace brought rejoicing. As various units arrived at the depots bound for Fort Oglethorpe and demobilization, enthusiasm soared, especially at times when returning veterans paraded through the streets. Finally, on July 4 a great peace pageant was staged at Warner Park and as a lasting memorial, the city voted to approve a bond issue for construction of the Soldiers and Sailors Memorial Auditorium. On November 11, 1922, a large crowd witnessed the laying of the cornerstone.

Into the Twenties

A variety of other long-range developments emerged from the war experience. The participation of women in the nation's defense gave new impetus to the older suffrage movement. Locally, there had been little support until 1911 when Catherine J. Wester and her cousin Margaret Ervin became devotees of the cause; through their efforts an equal rights association got a start.

In 1917 a state law made it possible for the town of Lookout Mountain to permit women to vote in municipal elections and to hold posts on the school board. Mrs. Newell Sanders, wife of the former U. S. Senator and leading Republican, is credited with being the first woman in Tennessee to vote when she cast a ballot in April of 1918; her daughter, Mrs. James Anderson, won a seat on

Tivoli Theater. When completed in 1921, the Tivoli was claimed to be the "finest little theater in the South." The city of Chattanooga bought the theater in 1976 and makes it available for use as a cultural center.

Newton Chevrolet Building, 329 Market Street. Originally this 1920s structure was a fine example of an elegant automobile showroom.

the school board. The franchise law, broadened to permit women to vote in all municipal and presidential elections, found some 2000 Hamilton women going to the polls in 1919. Their lively interest along with the leadership provided by Abbey Crawford Milton, a staunch suffragist, helped bring about Tennessee's ratification of the nineteenth amendment to the Constitution. Following this victory, Sadie Watson on February 1, 1922, assumed the duties of county register—the first woman to hold elective office in the county government. Four years later Sarah Frazier won a seat in the 65th General Assembly, the third woman to sit in the Legislature.

Young men had experimented with wireless telegraphy before the war, and military operators got experience and encouragement to continue this interest. Earl Winger and Norman A. Thomas on August 13, 1925, began commercial broadcasting from station WDOD in the Hotel Patten, making available an entirely new medium for entertainment, news, and public service programs.

World War I likewise developed into a proving period for aviation. Locally, fellows like George B. David, Carl Morefield, and Johnny Green built experimental craft to the delight of followers who gathered at an improvised airstrip along Rossville Boulevard. An ardent supporter who headed the chamber of commerce's aeronautics committee, John E. Lovell, had a hand in establishing a field in East Chattanooga in 1919 where in due time passenger and mail planes landed. This facility, called Marr Field, was the scene of several bad accidents, so the field was condemned. Lovell then went to work to raise the needed funds for a major development. He succeeded in winning the city's approval of a bond issue for the purchase of some 130 acres, the nucleus for modern Lovell Field which opened in 1930. Four years later an Eastern aircraft pioneered commercial flights into the area.

In Chattanooga, in addition to the Memorial Auditorium, a number of structures, now landmarks, changed the city's skyline. A brief sampling, incomplete and selected at random, includes: The Times Building (1892), the old Post Office (1895), Erlanger Hospital (1899), Carnegie Library (1905), City Hall (1907), Christ Episcopal Church (1908), Hotel Patten (1908), James Building, called the city's first skyscraper (1908), Central High School in Ridgedale

(1908), Southern Railway Terminal Station (1909), First Presbyterian Church (1910), Engel Stadium (1929), Hamilton County Courthouse, designed by R. H. Hunt (1913), John A. Patten Memorial Chapel (1919), Tivoli Theater (1921), Tennessee Power Company Building (1924), Maclellan Building (1924), the new Read House (1926), American National Bank Building (1928), Chattanooga Bank Building (1928), Ochs Memorial Temple (1928), and T. C. Thompson Children's Hospital (1929).

Another physical change required the tearing down of certain buildings. Chattanooga's Broad Street ended abruptly at 9th Street; to the south the state of Georgia owned many acres which it had acquired in connection with the building of the Western and Atlantic Railroad. A row of small shops faced the street, making it impossible for the city to open a thoroughfare leading to St. Elmo and Lookout Mountain. On the night of May 6, 1926, Commissioner Ed Bass with a wrecking crew bulldozed a passageway through these structures during an interval when Georgia had no injunction preventing such action. A car drove through the opening, thereby establishing the use of the land for a street. Although Georgia officials fumed, a permanent contract was negotiated. Then after many years, the state of Georgia sold its property holdings in the heart of Hamilton County's county seat.

To the Mountains

Long before Broad Street's extension to the south, hamlets had grown into good-sized villages at the foot of and atop Lookout Mountain. With the construction of the belt line railroad, Alton Park became an industrial and residential suburb before its 1929 annexation. On to the west, St. Elmo, named for Augusta Jane Evans Wilson's novel with its scenes based in the area at the foot of Lookout Mountain, grew up as a residential district at the time of the building of the inclines and the mountain developments. Here only the Chattanooga Medicine Company (Chattem) provided employment for any sizable number of employees. In 1905 St. Elmo incorporated in order to provide the best arrangement for public schools and in 1929 readily approved annexation to the city.

On the mountain a post office (Lookout Mountain, Tennessee) opened in 1867. Efforts to build tourist business speeded develop-

Carnegie Library (Old Library Building). From its opening in 1905 to 1940, it served as Chattanooga's public library.

ment and led to the organization of municipal government in 1899 when the population numbered about 450. The automobile provided the incentive for more real estate activity and the improvement of the Ochs Highway in 1930.

Before that day, O. B. Andrews and Garnett Carter planned the Fairyland community and opened the Inn. Here Carter invented the game of miniature golf and held the country's first Tom Thumb Tournament. To the south and beyond the county border into Georgia, the booming 1920s witnessed the construction of another splendid hotel and the opening of the Rock City Gardens in 1932. On another part of the mountain the spelunker, Leo Lambert, discovered the fascinating cavern and underground waterfall which he named for his wife and opened in June of 1930 as Ruby Falls.

The veteran businessman, promoter, and area booster, Charles E. James, had ideas for a neighboring mountain. Even as early as the 1880s and 1890s he was planning the building of Signal Point City on Walden Ridge. In 1911 he revived his dream by constructing a fashionable inn which opened in 1913 (now Alexian Brothers Rest Home) and a 13-mile streetcar line connecting the mountain-top to Chattanooga. Charlie James, it was said, ran the "catamount from his hiding place on Walden Ridge and founded there a city. . . ."

The automobile made mountain real estate very desirable. The inn expanded, a golf course was added, and on April 4, 1919, a charter was granted for the town which chose James its mayor until his death in 1925. Incorporation was necessary in order to pass an ordinance to keep roaming cattle from eating up the golf course grass and the lawns of the private homes. After World War II Signal Mountain expanded rapidly as a residential community, insisting that its rugged natural setting be preserved.

By the end of the third decade of the twentieth century the county census listed 159,497 persons of whom 22.7 percent were black. Following the constant pattern of the years, only one percent of the total was foreign-born. This purity of stock provided the basis for genuine pride in tradition and folkways and undoubtedly contributed to provincialism as well as homogeneity. The religious tone was one of conservative theology expressed by some through healing power, "unknown tongues," and the handling of snakes. A state ban on the teaching of the "forbidden doctrine" of evolution did not disturb many citizens, while numerous Hamiltonians in 1925 applauded the efforts of William Jennings Bryan in the neighboring town of Dayton. Since then a long public argument and law suit have focused attention on the controversial question of the teaching of the Bible in the public schools.

Depression

During the 1920s the county's economy tended to move toward the mainstream of American developments as units of national chain stores, services, and corporations moved here in growing numbers. But before the decade had run its course, such marginal activities as coal mining, textiles, and real estate experienced depression problems that already had marked the future of the 3838 persons engaged in agriculture.

As unemployment climbed and money grew tight, barter again came to the fore as a way of business. Chattanooga National Bank did not reopen after the bank holiday; mass meetings demanded reduced bus fares; vacant houses, it was said, along with other abandoned buildings were carried away for firewood. At Onion Bottom, Blue Goose Hollow, and Hell's Half Acre in Chattanooga people lived in pitiful poverty. "Hobo Jungles" sprouted along the railroads and under viaducts and from one of these depression camps the tragedy of the Scottsboro boys was spawned.

TVA

From such disheartening conditions came voters who helped elect Franklin D. Roosevelt president in 1932 as he called for relief, recovery, and reform. A keystone in his extensive program was the development of the Tennessee River. By May 18, 1933, he signed legislation creating the Tennessee Valley Authority, which was locally greeted by a "bedlam of noise." Then a mood of caution followed with outright criticism expressed by spokesmen who feared the old order was passing in favor of socialistic planning. The *Chattanooga News,* published by George Fort Milton, countered, "There is in prospect the greatest plan for social as well as economic reconstruction of a region ever undertaken. . . . The

Tennessee Valley will be Exhibit A of the new America." Milton was joined by former U. S. Senator William E. Brock in supporting TVA.

The multipurpose valley-wide project was designed to extract the maximum good from the currents of the Tennessee River and reduce its hurtful ways to a minimum; navigation, flood control, generation of electric energy, conservation by proper land usage were specific goals along with the design to improve the "economic and social well-being of the people living in said river basin."

A barrage of criticism and propaganda, most of which centered on the government's generation of power, swept across the nation. It reinforced the deepening split in Hamilton County. A map overlay of the valley placed across one of Tennessee reveals the shape of the TVA basin to be that of a butterfly with the body centered in the Chattanooga country. Not only was the region the geographic center of the great experiment but also it was home base for the Tennessee Electric Power Company (TEPCO), which served most of the valley as a private utility. Jo Conn Guild was its president within the holding company, Commonwealth and Southern, headed by Wendell Wilkie. Milton summed up these factors by saying that the region was "really the Hindenburg line of private power."

A citizens' council worked to locate a dam nearby, to acquire TVA offices locally, and to provide for a municipally-owned power distribution system in order to enjoy TVA rates. A dam within the county did not have TVA's priority rating at the time because the directors stressed the greater importance of tributary storage dams for control of potential flood waters, a fact that "soured" some local political leaders. But the big argument revolved around electric power. Public vs. private ownership arguments touched off serious debate which often degenerated into a display of prejudice and rumors of disaster.

The state government authorized a city referendum for March 12, 1935, providing for the sale of $8,000,000 in bonds to finance the acquisition of a municipal power distribution system which would then sell TVA current. The debate was no longer academic; for weeks it dominated the news. Tongues grew sharp; charges of fraud and counter charges added to the emotion of the hour.

Victory went by a wide margin to the supporters of public power, and the Chattanooga Electric Power Board came into being. Several years passed before the board rendered any service. Since TEPCO would not dispose of its system, the board was forced to begin construction of an expensive duplicate distribution facility. Eventually, Wilkie concluded that sale was inevitable, and all of TEPCO's properties were sold on August 15, 1939. For $10,850,000 the Power Board took over the so-called TEPCO's Chattanooga District, a service area which encompasses practically all of Hamilton County and portions of neighboring counties. In 1950 the board estimated that 95 percent of the people in this 500-square-mile territory had access to electricity. During the first year, the board had about 40,000 customers; at the end of 1979 it provided power for 120,342. The board pays large annual sums in lieu of taxes to both Chattanooga and Hamilton County; it is the largest "payer of taxes" to both units.

Another part of the TEPCO sale included TVA's purchase of the Hales Bar Lock and Dam and the steam plant. The Authority raised the level of this Marion County dam to meet its standard which called for a nine-foot channel across that part of Hamilton County downstream from Chickamauga Dam. At a later date Nickajack Dam replaced the older structure.

Determined political leaders, among them County Judge Will Cummings, Congressman Sam McReynolds, and U.S. Senators Kenneth McKeller and Nathan L. Bachman of Signal Mountain, constantly worked for a main river dam for Hamilton County. Finally, in August of 1935 they managed to have it placed on the TVA construction schedule. Whistles and bells again announced good tidings across the county: construction would lift the region from depression's firm grasp. Engineers and geologists made soundings; archaeologists hastily explored for Indian artifacts and fossils. About 60,000 acres of land were purchased. Construction, done by TVA work crews, cost approximately $39,000,000. On Labor Day of 1940 President Roosevelt visited the site to dedicate Chickamauga dam and lake.

The dam, 5800 feet in length, is 129 feet high with a normal lock lift of 51 feet. The lake covers 35,400 acres and is 58.9 miles long and actually reduces the size of the county from 576 to 550.4

square miles. Wolftever, Soddy, Sale, and Oppossum creeks became major embayments; the old Indian site at Dallas disappeared under the waters as did the former county seat of Harrison. The three original generating units had a capacity of 81,000 kilowatts, approximately Chattanooga's consumption in 1940. Twelve years later a fourth generator raised capacity to 108,000 kilowatts, but by this time the city's demand amounted to about triple this figure.

An entirely new life-style emerged along the 810 miles of shoreline which reached out in irregular patterns across the county and beyond to Watts Bar Dam. Rolling hillsides with their hardwood and evergreen coverings extending to the water's edge offered inviting sites for rustic homes, club facilities, marinas, campsites, and parklands. Water recreational activities with a great variety of supporting businesses and services gave Hamiltonians vacation lands at their doorstep.

World War II

President Roosevelt's dedicatory remarks contained reference to the European war crisis and to the role TVA might play in national defense. Before many months had passed, the Authority had to accelerate its construction schedule and expand its generating capacity to unanticipated wartime totals. The power division, located in Chattanooga, operated as a vital center for the swelling utility, pressed to provide power for war industries and for such mammoth projects as the one at Oak Ridge. The maps and survey division, also housed in Chattanooga, turned from valley mapping to doing more than one-half million square miles of enemy territory.

Hamilton County industry retooled for war by producing a variety of articles including blankets, textiles, artillery parts, shells, tanks, and steel alloy. The Chattanooga Medicine Company packaged "K" rations, and near Tyner some 7500 acres became the site of the Volunteer Ordnance Works, built in 1941–1942 and operated by the Hercules Powder Company.

Unlike World War I, no display of gaudy emotionalism was generated. The county sent 25, 258 men and women into military service of whom 695 did not return. To honor their role in the community effort a memorial in Patten Parkway, dedicated Febru-

Hamilton County Courthouse, a handsome building of Neo-classical design, completed in 1913. On the grounds are statues of Confederate General A. P. Stewart and John Ross, "Indian Chief, Loyal Cherokee, Great American." A six-story Criminal Justice Building is the latest addition to the courthouse

ary 22, 1950, reminds their peers and posterity of their contribution. One soldier, Technical Sergeant Charles H. Coolidge of
Signal Mountain, earned the Medal of Honor for his heroic con-
duct under duress.

As in other wars, uniformed personnel from Fort Oglethorpe,
joined this time by many from Camp Forrest, overwhelmed
downtown Chattanooga. But by January of 1943 a noticeable
change occurred; Fort Oglethorpe was designated the Third
Woman's Army Auxiliary Corps Training Center and merchants
had to stock their shelves with a different inventory. Following the
conflict, however, the military base in north Georgia was dismantled permanently on the last day of 1946.

Another Postwar Era

No decline in the demand for TVA power occurred after
demobilization and the Authority found itself the largest utility in
the country, but the continuing demand for energy required a shift
from dependence on hydroelectric generation to the use of steam
turbines. None of these giant fossil fuel plants were built in Hamilton County, but management of the entire system resided in Chattanooga. Many residents naturally became involved in the renewed
argument over government development of electric energy.

In addition to coal-burning plants TVA undertook a uniquely
designed experiment in 1970 along the Hamilton-Marion county
boundary line named the Raccoon Mountain Pumped-Storage
Hydro-Plant to produce "peak" period power. That same year the
Authority started work in the northern part of the county on the
expensive Sequoyah Nuclear Plant, designed to produce 2.5 million kilowatts. At maximum construction an estimated 2700 workers had employment at Sequoyah alone. In 1980 both projects
appear to be nearing an operational date.

Today TVA is challenged to lead experimentation in the national energy struggle, a role encouraged by its chairman S. David
Freeman, who spent his youth in Chattanooga. In the south central
business district of the city, plans are proceeding for the construction of an office complex and computer center designed to be the
"world's showplace for solar energy." Linked with a large package
of private developments—an office building, parking facility,

commercial hotel, and industrial trade center—this 20.2-acre redevelopment will represent a $200,000,000 modernization.
Meanwhile discussions over rates, nuclear safety, and conservation
go on.

Over the years TVA's less glamorous functions also have altered
quietly the face of Hamilton County. Farm woodlots and forest
areas responded to scientific forestry practices and tree harvesting.
Many acres of waste and idle land have been planted in fast-
growing trees. Although much agricultural land has been crowded
out of cultivation by subdivisions, shopping centers, and rural
commercial enterprises, the average size of the county farms has
increased as the number has declined. The source of income has
changed; about 75 percent in recent years has been generated
from milk, poultry, and livestock. Pastures and soybeans have taken
over the fields and in 1970 the county ranked third in the state in
egg production and seventh in broilers.

On the river, powerful tugs with utilitarian barges replaced the
romantic packets. Shipments of grain, soybeans, gravel, sand, fuel
oil, iron-steel products use the 650-mile nine-foot channel in all
seasons as do the massive nuclear components from Combustion
Engineering Company. The Tennessee–Tombigbee Waterway,
started in 1972, promises the fulfillment of an old dream of a
short-cut to the Gulf of Mexico, first tried in the Muscle Shoals
canals.

Passenger business had long vanished from the river and fast
declined on the railroads. On August 4, 1970, the *Birmingham
Special* made its last stop at the Terminal Station and on May 1,
1971, the L & N's *Georgian* completed its last run, ending all rail
passenger service. Privately-owned automobiles, interstate buses,
and commercial aviation had vanquished the "iron horse."

By the 1950s the local interstate highways—with such unimagi-
native names as I-75, I-24, I-124, I-59—gave the motor car all the
competitive advantages. Racing across Hamilton County is an end-
less caravan of many designs, colors, and license tags, for more than
one-half of America's population live within a day's drive. So
tourism continues as a major commercial activity; the scenery,
historic sites, and natural attractions which draw the traveler here
translate into a $188,000,000 business in the county annually.

Patten Parkway Historic District. *Courtesy of Chattanooga-Hamilton County Historic Advisory Board.*

In the expanding post World War II economy, manufacturing remains the area's prime occupation, revealing a constant trend toward firms with nonlocal headquarters. In 1977, of the companies employing more than 200 persons, 31 had their headquarters elsewhere, and 16 were homebased. Combustion Engineering and the Du Pont Textile Fibers plant employed the largest number of workers who, like other employees, commute from all corners of the county and beyond. Many live on farm places and raise livestock or carry on small-scale agriculture as a second source of income.

Mid-century technology produced an entirely new business opportunity which soon had a rippling effect in retail and service outlets. Broadcast television, pioneered by WDEF's Channel 12, signed on the air on April 25, 1954. Channels three and nine followed shortly after to be joined by a public broadcasting unit, Channel 45, in 1970.

In the field of the printed word, the *Chattanooga News-Free Press* acquired a growing list of subscribers to whom it presents conservative editorial and leadership policy. A product of the Depression, it began as a weekly throw-away carrying advertisement material for the food stores of Roy McDonald. On August 31, 1936, McDonald published, under the name *Free Press*, the first daily edition. Three years later he acquired the *Chattanooga News* and renamed the journal *Chattanooga News-Free Press*. Cooperative publishing arrangements with the older *Chattanooga Times* were followed for some years but gave way to a lively competition until a 1980 announced arrangement again promises joint business operations.

The national trend toward consolidation persisted in leaving its mark on the local economy. New organizations moved in while others, including an insurance home office and Coca-Cola Bottling Company (Thomas), relocated elsewhere. By 1978 the assessed value of property in the county passed $1,474,000,000 and over 600 manufacturing plants employed 57,300 persons. Although the bankruptcy of Hamilton Bancshares rocked the financial structure, six major banks and three federal and loan associations, of which First Federal is the oldest and largest, function as a barometer of the financial health of the area.

Education, Health, and Cultural Affairs

The merger concept and steady growth also involved higher education. The University of Chattanooga and Chattanooga City College, an institution for blacks, became a major campus of the state university in July of 1969. Under the name University of Tennessee at Chattanooga (UTC), an era of accelerated growth in the student body, expansion of campus facilities, and developing curriculum marked its first decade.

Southern Missionary College also experienced a period of expanded service by enrolling almost 2000 students. Another church-related institution of higher education got a start in the postwar years. On July 3, 1946, the Highland Park Baptist Church voted to sponsor a Bible school and junior college and added a senior college division plus graduate work before changing its name in 1979 to Tennessee Temple University. In 1977–1978 it enrolled over 3700 students.

Two state schools also came into existence in this same era. Students enrolled at the Chattanooga Area Vocational-Technical School in 1970. Five years earlier a two-year college-level program was implemented at Chattanooga State Technical Institute which moved to a campus on Amnicola Highway in 1967 and switched to the name Chattanooga State Technical Community College in 1973.

Cultural organizations and health care groups enjoyed years of prosperity comparable to those in education. Medical science had an extremely long way to go to attain the current standards of excellence. In 1941 Chattanooga and Hamilton County consolidated their health units under Dr. F. O. Pearson which led 20 years later to the opening of their joint health department building and to future branch offices and mobile service. Erlanger Hospital expanded constantly from its meager beginnings and in 1979 the city and county turned over responsibility for its operation to a hospital authority empowered to sell bonds and plan systematically for future expansion and modernization. In addition to small clinics offering personalized service, the area's facilities include: Memorial Hospital, operated by the Sisters of Charity of Nazareth, Kentucky (1952); the state's Moccasin Bend Psychiatric Hospital (1961); the Downtown General Hospital (originally built in 1908 and sold to Health Care, Incorporated, in 1969); Parkridge Hospital (1971); the East Ridge Community Hospital (1974); and the Red Bank Community Hospital (1977).

Two special projects have won national and international recognition for their service in treating and training physically and mentally handicapped persons: the Rehabilitation Center of the Siskin Memorial Foundation, established in 1950, specializing in physical therapy and dental clinics and speech and hearing programs; and Orange Grove School, which from small beginnings in 1953 has now grown into a modern center enrolling some 700 retarded students in classes, day care programs, and sheltered workshops.

Diverse groups and individuals, amateurs and professionals, provided an attractive array of talent in the creative arts. An early art association fell heir to the Bluff View home of George Hunter which was renovated and enlarged in 1970 for permanent and visiting collections. Directly across the Tennessee River the Little Theater constructed a building in 1962. The Chattanooga Symphony Orchestra (1934) and the Chattanooga Opera Association (1943) make use of the unusually good facilities of the city-owned Tivoli Theater. Numerous dance and music groups, the Boys' Choir, and the Festival Players supplement the organized programs of the schools, colleges, and churches of the county. Treasures of the past are on display at the Houston Antique Museum, the Tennessee Valley Railroad Museum, and the Chattanooga Museum of Regional History.

The many cultural activities get their support from individuals and from local foundations which generously fund educational, welfare, and health care projects as well. Such philanthropic aid is supplemented by money from the United Fund of Greater Chattanooga which has never failed in 58 years to meet its annual goal—a national record. As in health care, the city and county joined forces in supporting the Bicentennial Library. Dating back to the Carnegie Library of 1905, the new facility, dedicated in 1976, contains about 300,000 volumes.

A sampling of the individuals, Hamiltonians by birth or adoption, who have brought special credit to their homeland and acclaim to themselves includes; Estes Kefauver, U.S. senator and 1956 vice-presidential candidate; William E. Brock III, U.S. senator and chairman of the national Republican party; Lawrence Derthick, U.S. commissioner of education; Grace Moore, screen, Broadway, and grand opera star; Ralph McGill, editor of the *Atlanta Constitution;* S. David Freeman, chairman of the board of directors, Tennessee Valley Authority; Frank Wilson, federal judge; Adolph S. Ochs, publisher of the *New York Times*; Irvine Grote, consultant in chemical pharmacology; Ellis Meacham, author of sea adventure novels; Marilyn Lloyd Bouchard, present congressional representative and first woman representative from this district; Beverly Hilowitz, publisher, American Heritage Publishing Company; the Govan family (Gilbert, Christine, their daughters Emmy West and Mary Steele and son-in-law William O. Steele), authors; Alexander Guerry, educator; Paul Ramsey, poet; George Cress, painter and teacher; Harold Cadek, musician; and Harold Cash, sculptor.

Problems of the City

Since mid-century an aroused public conscience has focused national attention on diverse socio-economic problems and on crusades demanding equal democratic rights for all. These same issues with particular local characteristics obviously surfaced in Hamilton County, but since most were directly associated with city life, they chiefly became the problems of mayors P. R. Olgiati, Ralph Kelley, Robert Kirk Walker, and Pat Rose.

One complex matter related to environmental pollution. The concentration of industry within the city where a combination of geographic and meteorological conditions combined with a practice of using bituminous coal for home heating made Chattanooga one of the country's dirty cities. Early recognition of this condition led to no positive solution, while the mortality figures for tuberculosis told a grim tale. Following World War II, under government prodding, action produced corrective ordinances and a watchdog bureau to carry out the mandate. Early progress saw remarkable changes and Chattanooga won national acclaim for its efforts. However, enforcement frequently was weakened because of divided local, state, and national authority and industrial resistance. Pockets of suspended particulate still exist, bad atmospheric conditions periodically downgrade the air quality, but the 20-person bureau feels that considerable progress has been made. Fortunate for all residents is the fact that within a few miles of the core city, parklands have been reserved where the air is fresh and clean. In 1940 the state secured two sites on Lake Chickamauga: Harrison Bay State Park and Booker T. Washington State Park, which, because of the war, were not formally opened until July of 1950. Near the dam TVA maintains a swimming and recreational area and across the lake the county supports the Chester Frost Park. Along South Chickamauga Creek is found Audubon Acres with its many trails and rich natural setting while on the west slope of Lookout Mountain has been established the Chattanooga Nature Center and Reflection Riding on 375 acres of botanical and historic lands. Closer to the city can be seen the wildlife refuge on Maclellan Island and the cooperatively-owned Moccasin Bend, which the city and county reserve for public use. A few miles beyond stand the 35,000 acres of the Prentice Cooper State Forest and Wildlife Management Area developed by the state along the Marion-Hamilton county line.

A second complicated matter involves racial relations. After the adoption of the mayor-commission form of government in 1911 with its city-wide elections, no black won a commission seat until John P. Franklin's victory in 1971. In the years following World War I some advances had been achieved in an interracial movement and the city in conjunction with the county established Lincoln Park. Moreover, the black community was not without some political voice, and Walter C. Robinson emerged as one of the Negroes' most influential political leaders in the city's history. The National Urban League in 1947 pursuant to a local survey stated that, despite specific shortcomings, there was real cooperation between the races. But it was not until reapportionment became a reality that the area returned Clarence B. Robinson to the state assembly in 1974.

Gradual change and paternalistic practices, however, had not challenged the fundamental social questions represented by the Jim Crow laws. In the 1950s a new spirit of revolt generated by supreme court decisions and federal-state civil rights legislation took root in the nation, and Chattanooga reacted as did other cities. Implementation of the 1954 desegregation orders produced fear, turmoil, and violence. At the first citizens' meeting on the school issue someone dropped a teargas vial; postponement of any action was taken immediately.

A brawl at the auditorium in 1958 which nurtured racial overtones rocked the community. February of 1960 "sit-downs" at lunch counters set off explosive confrontations and the next year theater "stand-ins" continued to signal a divided community. From such incidents the city recovered its poise through the efforts of interracial citizens' groups and governmental officials under the leadership of William E. Brock, Jr. An ordinance adopted September 24, 1963, announced that "all facilities of the city of Chattanooga are open to all citizens." This reaffirmed such decisions as the use of the library, parks, golf course, and auditorium. Most commercial facilities also acknowledged the "right" of all persons to use their establishments although patronage was light for some years.

The postponed consideration of desegregated schools led to a suit which brought on an announced limited plan to begin on September 5, 1962. That year 44 blacks attended six formerly white city schools, and Hamilton County voluntarily followed a similar design. By 1966 both systems had legally ended the practice of separate schools, but the "mix" did not reveal a thorough integration. Trivial incidents at two high schools, the use of the song "Dixie" and of the Confederate flag, led to scuffles in the schools that escalated into the community. In 1971 the U.S. Supreme Court ordered "all vestiges" of segregation removed and approved busing as a method of obtaining this goal. On May 22, 1971, violence erupted. Night curfews did not bring calm; airlines canceled night flights; industry adjusted its shifts. Some 2000 National Guardsmen were brought into the city to preserve order. Arson was practiced; one man died of gunshot wounds. Only after about a week's time did tension ease.

Another school year loomed in September with new arrangements based on pairing and clustering of schools and on busing. But the stormy era was passing and the bus program was implemented with apprehension but without further violence. The presence of John Franklin as commissioner of education and of C. C. Bond as assistant superintendent of city schools helped to avoid further racial scars. By-products of this era of desegregation of the schools have been the phenomenal growth of independent schools unrelated to public support and the movement of many whites to suburban areas and beyond.

Business moved with this exodus, and the national trend of creating shopping centers was repeated at Brainerd Village (1960), Eastgate (1961), Northgate (1972), and numerous smaller places. These developments noticeably hastened the deterioration of the inner city where islands of deplorable housing had long existed. In 1951 Mayor P. R. Olgiati took office and accepted the challenge of revitalizing the city which was no easy matter: freeways, a river bridge, railroad relocation, slum clearance, an interceptor sewer system, and public opinion could not be separated one from the other.

Central to planning was the Golden Gateway Redevelopment Project comprising about 403 acres of the dying west side. Here 1400 families had to be relocated, 1170 buildings razed, and the top

Fountain Square Historic District. The buildings in this district show architectural trends from 1900 to 1928.

of Cameron Hill removed despite the cries of history buffs in order to provide dirt for the interstate system. Eventually the cleared acreage became private property; the YMCA (1969), First Baptist Church (1967), St. Barnabas Nursing Home and Apartment complex (1965–1966), and the Jaycee Towers I and II (1970, 1975) set standards for the planned renewal which was completed in December of 1976.

Cooperative plans and implementation to relocate downtown railroad tracks, yards, and street crossings required more than a decade. It meant in part the construction of L & N yards in the valley of Lookout Creek, the rechanneling of portions of Chattanooga Creek, and the building of rail bridges over certain streets. This huge package, labeled Chattanooga Runaround, was finished in 1972 and was soon followed by the sale of the railroad lands in the downtown section of the city by the state of Georgia.

All this had an invigorating effect on the core city. Wise land use, systematic planning, and modern architecture offered a fresh appearance to the changing skyline. Representative of the new structures are the Hamilton County Justice Building (1976), the Civic Forum (1979), the Chattanooga-Hamilton County Bicentennial Library (1976), the Krystal Building (1978), the enlarged Provident Building (1976), Blue Cross-Blue Shield (1971), the Commerce Union Bank Towers I and II (1974–1978), First Federal Savings & Loan (1979), and the TVA Federal Credit Union building (1978).

Restored old structures and new parks aided in providing an openness to the new downtown. Some of the renovations are the Tivoli Theater, the Choo-Choo, the Times Building, Patten Towers, Park Plaza, and the Sports Barn. The recreation areas include John Ross Landing Park by the river, Miller Park in the heart of town, Market Center with its plazas and plantings, and the miniature Boynton Park. Unfortunately, renewal does not embrace everything; deteriorating buildings, some burned-out hulks, newly exposed walls, and unsightly parking areas are reminders that the struggle for renaissance is never-ending.

The upgrading of contiguous neighborhoods by governmental and private sponsorship has followed the rejuvenation of downtown. Highland Park, Orchard Knob, East Lake, the Third

Street district, Fountain Square, and Fort Wood are examples. Today community leaders are watching very carefully the projected plans for the south central city as well as tentative plans for East Ninth Street.

Another major municipal problem has worried political leaders. Not only had the city stood still in size and population for the past 25 years but large numbers of suburban commuters used city services without contributing to the community's income. This mushrooming growth beyond the city limits again invited annexation with its prospects for additional taxes and for increases in state and national appropriations based on population.

A new state law passed in 1955 paved the way for such action; it permitted cities to extend their borders by simple ordinance without the consent of the people of an annexed area and without any public hearing. Moreover, the task of proving any annexation to be unreasonable rested on the affected citizens. Residents, however, in the outlying districts who did not want to pay city taxes showed their rage, and a long, hectic battle took place.

Chattanooga at once began to plan to annex certain areas. The first places involved Eastdale, Sequoia-Woodmore, Spring Creek, and parts of East Brainerd. Lawsuits brought postponement of final action, but within a few years the city government announced a second round of annexations. Major industries within the region objected; echoes of black opposition, fearful of a loss of political power within the city, joined the chorus of protest.

A more palatable plan was offered to the concerned citizens consisting of a "variable tax," partial city services and partial taxes paid. This action only quelled opposition until the law was declared unconstitutional. After another season of protest and litigation, Amnicola, Stuart Heights, Tyner-Hawkinsville, Lake Hills, Murray Hills, and another part of East Brainerd came under Chattanooga's umbrella.

By February of 1972 the city proceeded to take in additional large tracts: North Hixson, Signal Hills, Middle Valley, Gold Point, King's Point-McCarty, the rest of East Brainerd, Tyner-Hawkinsville, Wauhatchie, North Mountain Creek, and Tiftonia. Legal processes in opposition were exhausted finally in July of 1974. According to Mayor Walker, the city now had a population of

166,200 persons living within its 118.6 square miles. Since that time growth has been slow.

The friends of annexation rejoiced, but many of the new citizens harbored hostile feelings, especially when services were slow in forthcoming. The transfer of school properties from county to city meant a complex contest over compensation which is still unresolved. Within the extended city borders kudzu and blackberries grow lush, ditches fill with summer weeds, which do cover up some of the roadside litter, and the city fathers argue about the use of steel traps for furbearing animals within the corporate limits.

Incorporation

Some of the outlying regions with concentrated populations avoided annexation because they had formerly incorporated or did so in the face of union with Chattanooga. Wedged between the city and the Georgia state line, the town of East Ridge incorporated in 1921 when it contained only about 300 residents. The opening of the Bachman tubes in 1928 combined with the promotional work of Weldon F. Osborne spurred growth. Today about 25,000 people live in this residential, commercial suburb which, with the construction of the interstate highways, has become a motel haven, inheriting a variety of highway problems. In 1957 and 1959 the people voted in heated contests against joining Chattanooga.

Lookout Mountain, Tennessee, which incorporated as early as 1890, occupies a tightly restricted area on the mountaintop north of the Georgia border. With motor transportation shrinking the eight-mile trip to the city, this desirable home-site district developed fast. Residents today share the panoramic scenery with a tourist industry which fills the highways and byways throughout the year.

Ridgeside (Shepherd Hills) incorporated in 1931 after voting against an annexation referendum, 38 to 14. In the 1970s this small island of private homes completely surrounded by Chattanooga contained about 400 residents.

In contrast to the communities of Lookout Mountain and Ridgeside, the town of Signal Mountain mushroomed after World War II to an estimated 5187 residents. The community, early developed by Charles James, incorporated in 1919. Within its

Federal Building. The U. S. Post Office and Courthouse, constructed in 1932, is the best local example of Art Deco architecture.

borders can be found orchid-growing establishments and the Alexian Brothers Rest Home, but it supports no industry. As a middle-class residential suburb, the town emphasizes careful preservation of its natural surroundings.

A post office established in 1881 to serve an area north of the river was first named Pleasant Hill; but because Tennessee already had a locality with this name, a second choice had to be made. The postmaster and his wife selected Red Bank, which remained a rural hamlet until an interurban streetcar line gave it direct access to Chattanooga after World War I. A few new stores opened, more modest homes were constructed, and some residents toyed with the idea of renaming the place Daytonia.

Before long the advantages of incorporation caught the attention of some leaders of Red Bank, who were joined in this movement by voters in nearby White Oak. The state annexation law spurred them on and, to avoid possible incorporation into Chattanooga, the people of the two towns voted on June 21, 1955, to form the town of Red Bank-White Oak. Steady expansion in apartment housing helped to increase the population to some 15,000, while in 1967 it was officially decided to drop the clumsy hyphenated name for the simpler designation, Red Bank.

In another part of the county the people of Collegedale voted 216 to 74 in November of 1968 to form their own government. Most of the 3000 residents are associated with the Southern Missionary College and the McKee Baking Company. The decision to incorporate in part resulted from a desire to avoid merging with Chattanooga; they not only wanted to steer clear of urban taxes but also to remain beyond reach of the city's Sunday ordinances, which would run directly counter to the lifestyle of this Seventh Day Adventist community.

The old Hamilton communities of Soddy and Daisy had relied on an economic base of coal, coke, and tile before the Depression. After World War II the motor car and good roads helped bring a new spirit to the area, and it was at that time that it experienced its greatest growth. In 1969 a very large acreage along the highway incorporated as Soddy-Daisy to preserve political independence. The following year the census reported 7569 residents. All continue to rejoice at the success of their town and boast of its debt-free operations.

Two mini-cities, Lakesite in 1972 and Walden in 1975, organized their own governments. Both remain very small residential areas whose citizens appear to enjoy the opportunity to participate in self-rule.

In addition to Hamilton's 10 municipalities, a number of small unincorporated communities dot the countryside. At least two, Ooltewah and Apison, considered incorporation but shied away for financial reasons. Harrison, the old county seat, Summit, Snow Hill, Grasshopper, Birchwood, Ryall Springs, Falling Water, Sawyer, Mowbray, Bakewell, Sale Creek, Coulterville, and others illustrate the wide variety of village life.

County Government

The direct relation of these people with government is with the county, where for years Judges Will Cummings, Wiley O. Couch, and Wilkes T. Thrasher, Sr., exercised strong leadership. In 1941 the Legislature prescribed a basic change in the structure of the county administration when it established a council of four part-time members and a manager. The quarterly court which for years had wielded political clout and governmental power suddenly found its authority so eroded as to be almost negligible, but local government rocked along much as always with a two-party rivalry keeping elections lively.

Then came the impact of the U.S. Supreme Court decision popularly referred to as "one man one vote," which grew out of Tennessee's failure to reapportion its Legislature according to constitutional obligation. In 1950, for example, the county had only three members of the lower house of the six to which it was entitled. Moreover, a decision that single district elections had to be held opened the way for the election of more Republicans in Hamilton County and more blacks.

On the state level, Hamilton gave the Republicans a resounding victory and sent Clarence B. Robinson to the House in 1974 as the first black member since the Reconstruction days of Hodge and Hutchins. The question about neglected reapportionment also arose on the county level. There was no doubt about needed

Ferger Place Historic District. *Courtesy of Chattanooga-Hamilton County Historic Advisory Board.*

reform, but when the two parties both undertook to redraw district lines, they accused each other of political and racial gerrymandering. When it was all said and done, the Republicans controlled the defunct court on which two women and two blacks now sat.

The local furor quickly subsided when, as a result of a state constitutional convention's revision of the county government act and its later ratification by the state voters, Hamilton got an entirely new form of local government although the county electorate voted against the new arrangement. This provided for a board of commissioners to replace both the county court and the county council. Nine part-time commissioners elected from districts were designated a legislative body while a county executive replaced the county judge as chief administrator. On September 1, 1978, the new model government assumed power without precedent or clear definition of duties. Both old and new political figures sat on the board, which comprised eight Democrats and one Republican of

Kelley House. *Courtesy of Chattanooga-Hamilton County Historic Advisory Board.*

whom two are blacks and one is a woman; Dalton Roberts became the first executive.

Metro

During the turbulent years of annexation and the demise of Jim Crow legislation, some Hamiltonians found the popular new concept of metropolitan government to their liking. They would challenge the old system and scrap both county and city government for a single new political organization. This approach was legally possible in Tennessee; Nashville and Davidson County already had approved consolidation while the people of Memphis and Knoxville had defeated it.

In 1962 the local effort got under way and, amid much publicity and deliberate consideration, a charter was prepared for public perusal. Concurrent majorities within the city and within the remaining county area had to approve this framework of government in a special referendum. The residents of Hamilton went to the polls on April 28, 1964, but turned down the proposal. They had been successfully swayed by the opposition's cry of possible tax increases and city dictatorship.

By August 6, 1970, the metro supporters were ready for another try after receiving endorsements from prominent politicians and both newspapers. Chattanooga's blacks worked to defeat a new charter: they feared they would lose some of their newly-won political advantages. The school busing issue surfaced as another cogent reason for opposing a new form of government. This time Chattanooga approved consolidation but the people living beyond the corporate limits again defeated it by 2280 votes.

The mountains continue their silent watch over the destiny of the area, but the winds of change ever blow, signaling a need to be alert to the old order.

Suggested Readings

Abshire, David M. *The South Rejects a Prophet: The Life of Senator D. M. Key, 1824–1900.* New York: Praeger, 1967.

Armstrong, Zella. *History of Hamilton County and Chattanooga Tennessee.* 2 vols., Chattanooga: Lookout Publishing Company, 1931–1940.

Brown, John P. *Old Frontiers: The Story of the Cherokee Indians from Earliest Times to the Date of Their Removal to the West.* Kingsport: Southern Publishers, 1938. (Reprint edition by Arno Press, 1971.)

Campbell, Thomas J. *The Upper Tennessee.* Chattanooga: T. J. Campbell, 1932.

Cartwright, Joseph H. *The Triumph of Jim Crow: Tennessee Race Relations in the 1880s.* Knoxville: University of Tennessee Press, 1976.

Catton, Bruce. *Never Call Retreat.* (volume 3, The Centennial History of the Civil War) Garden City: Doubleday & Company, 1965.

Davidson, Donald. *The Tennessee The Old River: Frontier to Secession.* New York: Rinehart & Company, 1946. (Reprint edition by University of Tennessee Press, 1978.)

Foreman, Grant. *Indian Removal: Emigration of the Five Civilized Tribes of Indians.* Norman: University of Oklahoma Press, 1932

———. *Sequoyah.* Norman: University of Oklahoma Press, 1938, 1959.

Govan, G. E. and Livingood, J. W. *The Chattanooga Country: From Tomahawks to TVA 1540–1976.* 3rd ed. Knoxville: University of Tennessee Press, 1977.

Johnson, Gerald W. *An Honorable Titan: A Biographical Study of Adolph S. Ochs.* New York: Harper & Brothers, 1946.

Johnson, Leland R. *Engineers on the Twin Rivers: A History of the Nashville District Corps of Engineers United States Army.* Nashville: U.S. Army Engineer District, 1978.

Lamon, Lester C. *Black Tennesseans, 1900–1930.* Knoxville: University of Tennessee Press, 1977.

Lewis, T.M.N. and Kneberg, Madeline. *Tribes That Slumber: Indians of the Tennessee Region.* Knoxville: University of Tennessee Press, 1958.

McCraw, Thomas K. *TVA and the Power Fight, 1933–1939.* Philadelphia: Lippincott, 1971.

Mooney, James. "Myths of the Cherokees," *19th Annual Report*, U.S. Bureau of American Ethnology. Washington: GPO, 1900. (Reprint edition by Johnson Reprint Corp., 1970.)

Moulton, Gary E. *John Ross: Cherokee Chief*. Athens: University of Georgia Press, 1978.

Patten, Cartter. *Signal Mountain and Walden's Ridge*. Chattanooga: The Author, 1961.

Peacock, Mary Thomas. *The Circuit Rider and Those Who Followed, Sketches of Methodist Churches Organized before 1860 in the Chattanooga Area* . . . . Chattanooga: Hudson, 1957.

Tucker, Glenn. *Chickamauga: Bloody Battle in the West*. Indianapolis: Bobbs-Merrill, 1961.

Walker, Robert Sparks. *Lookout: The Story of a Mountain*. Kingsport: Southern, 1941.

————. *Torchlights to the Cherokee: The Brainerd Mission*. New York: Macmillan, 1931.

Wilson, John. *Lookout: The Story of an Amazing Mountain*. Chattanooga: News-Free Press, 1977.

Woodward, Grace S. *The Cherokees*. Norman: University of Oklahoma Press, 1963.

Index

Academies, *see* Schools and colleges
Aetna Mountain, 3, 31
Agriculture, 29, 59, 74, 94, 100–101; *see* Farms and farming
Airports, 90; *see* Transportation
Alabama, 12, 57
Alabama and Chattanooga Railroad, 57
Aldehoff's School, 38
Alexian Brothers Rest Home, 93, 113
Allison, M. M., 86
Alpine Academy, 38
Alton Park, community of, 81, 91
American Board of Commissioners for Foreign Missions, 13–14
American Federation of Labor, 82
American Missionary Association, 71
American National Bank Building, 91
American Revolution, 9, 11, 19
American Trust and Banking Company, 87
Amnicola, community of, 81, 110
Annexation, 81, 91, 110–111, 113
Anderson, Mrs. James, 88, 90
Anderson Pike, 30, 44
Andrews, Garnett, Jr., 82
Andrews, James, 42
Andrews, O. B., 93
Apison, community of, 114
Appalachian Mountains, 12
Appomattox, 71
Archaeologists, 96; sites, 6–7
Archaic Period, 6
Architects, in county, 74, 91
Architecture, in city, 109
Armstrong, Martin, 19
Artists, in county, 74, 104; gallery, 103
Asbury United Methodist Church, (picture) 37
Atlanta Constitution, 104
Atlanta, Ga., 29, 45, 59, 82
Atlas, the, 25
Audubon Acres, 105

Authors, in county, 74, 104
Automobiles, 86, 93, 100, 104, 113; races, 86; *see* Transportation
Avalon, the 67
Aviation, 90, 100, 107
Avondale Community, 81

Bachman, Jonathan W., 53
Bachman, Nathan L., 96
Bachman tunnel, 111; *see* Tunnels
Bakewell, community of, 114
Bakewell Mountain, 5
Banks, in county, 30, 87, 94
Baptists, 23, 37; *see* Religion
Baptist Church, 45; *see* Churches
Bass, Ed, 91
Battle of Chickamauga, 44
Battle of Wauhatchie, 45
Bauxite ridge, 3
Baylor, J. Roy, 73
Baylor School, 73
Bell, John, 38
Bernhardt, Sarah, 62
Berry, James, 29
Birmingham, Al., 57
Birmingham Special, the, 100
Birchwood Community, 38, 72, 114
Blacks, in county, 14, 22, 33, 37–38, 45, 49, 51, 71–74, 76–81, 93, 102, 106–107, 114–117
Blacksmiths, in county, 22, 30
Blast furnace, 37
Bledsoe Company, 22
Blount, Alfred, 79
Blue Goose Hollow Community, 94
Blue Cross-Blue Shield, 109
Bluff Furnace, (picture) 26, 39
Bluff View, home of George Hunter, 103
Board of Trade, 59
Boats, 17, 27, 29, 30, 57, 100; *see* Steamboats, Packets
Bond, C. C., 107

121

Monroe, James, 15
Montague, Theodore G., 51, 87
Moravians, 13
Morefield, Carl, 90
Morris Plan Bank, 87
Motel, 111
Mountain Creek, 5, 22
Mount Bethel Church, 23
Mowbray, community of, 114
Murray Hill, community of, 110
Muscle Shoals, 25, 100
Museums, 65, 104
Musicians, 75, 104

Narrows, the, 3, 11, 25
Nashville and Chattanooga Railroad,
    30–31; and St. Louis, 59
Nashborough, 10
Nashville, city of, 31, 42
National Urban League, 106
Navigation, 3, 8, 10, 25
Negro Congregational Church, 71
New England, 14
New Muscle Shoals Canal, 57
New Opera House Company, 62
New Orleans, 8
Newspapers, 15, 28, 39, 42, 46, 56,
    61–62, 64–65, 66, 74, 78, 86–87, 94,
    102, 117
Newton Chevrolet Building, (picture) 89
New York, 71, 85; Broadway in, 75
New York Peace Monument, 65
New York Times, the, 65–66, 104
Nickajack Dam, 96; Road, 13; Trace, 8
Nicklin, John B., 51
North Carolina, 7, 10–11, 19, 25
North Chattanooga, 73, 81
North Chickamauga Creek, 5, 20
Northgate, 107
North Hixson, community of, 110
North Mountain Creek, 110
Notre Dame school, 72
Nuclear energy, 100

Oak Grove Park, 81
Oak Grove School, 103
Oak Ridge, 97
Ochs, Adolph S., 62–66, 104
Ochs Highway, 93

Ochs Memorial Temple, 91
Ocoee Land District, 25, 29, 38
Ocoee River, 86
Olgiati, P. R., 105, 107
Onion Bottom, community of, 94
Ooltewah, 8, 47, 49, 114; Gap, 3
Oppossum, 97
Orange Grove, 81
Orchard Knob, 63, 66, 81, 109
Ore, James, 12
Osborne, Weldon F., 111
Our Southern Birds, 74
Overhill Cherokee, 7, 9

Packets, 67; *see* boats
Paleo Age, 6
Parden, Noah W., 79
Pardo, Juan, 7
Parham, Ferdinand, 27–28
Parham, Katie, 51
Parham, Louis L., 74
Park Plaza, 109
Parkridge Hospital, 103
Parks, 43, 63–67, 69, 71, 76, 81, 97,
    105–106, 109
Paterson, Robert, 23
Patten Hotel, 90
Patten, John A., 67, 85; Memorial
    Chapel, 91
Patten Parkway Historic District, 97,
    (picture) 101
Patten Towers, 109
Patten, Z. C., 51, 82
Patterson, Robert, 21
Payne, T. H., 51
Pearson, A. A., 41
Pearson, F. O., 103
Peyton, Mrs. Ephraim, 10
Philanthropic organizations, 104
Phosphorous, 57
Pioneer Bank, 87
Pine Hill, 3
Pleasant Hill, 113
Poets, 74, 104
Point Lookout, 69, 71
Political parties, 9, 38, 47, 49, 53, 55–56,
    71, 78, 88, 104, 114–115
Pollution, 105
Possum Creek, 5

About the Author

James Weston Livingood, a native of Birdsboro, Pennsylvania, came to Chattanooga and Hamilton County after receiving a B. S. degree from Gettysburg College and M.A. and Ph.D. degrees from Princeton University. His interest in regional history has been evident throughout his tenure at the University of Tennessee at Chattanooga where he has served as professor, dean of arts and sciences, dean of the university, and distinguished research professor of history. He has been active in local, regional, state, and national historical societies and organizations. As emeritus professor, he has continued his research and prolific writing.

Among his numerous published works are *The University of Chattanooga: Sixty Years; The Chattanooga Country: From Tomahawks to TVA,* with Gilbert E. Govan; and with J. Leonard Raulston, *Sequachie: A Story of the Southern Cumberlands.* He has completed a comprehensive history of Hamilton County, which is forthcoming from Memphis State University Press. Additionally, he has contributed to *Landmarks of Tennessee History,* Colliers, Americana, and Britannica encyclopedias and has had articles published in *Saturday Review, Chattanooga Times,* and historical journals.